Fortress Storming

by John Burke

**Masters Series
Guide to Kata & Bunkai**

Karate Academy
- 2012 -

© Martial Arts World Ltd 2005, John Burke 2012

First published in Great Britain in 2005 by
Martial Arts World Ltd,
Newton Abbot, Devon, TQ12 2RX

This edition
Karate Academy, Newton Abbot, Devon, TQ12 4PB

Fortress Storming
By John Burke

Published by
Karate Academy
8, Signal Buildings, Brunel Road, Newton Abbot, Devon, TQ12 4PB, England

Printed and Bound in Great Britain.

British Library Cataloguing in Publication
Data available

ISBN 0-9550340-0-0

Warning:
Martial Arts can be dangerous. Practice should not be undertaken without first consulting your physician. Training should take place under the supervision of a qualified instructor. The contents of this book are for educational use and in no way do we endorse the use of the techniques herein. Practitioners need to be aware of the Law and how it pertains to "Use of Reasonable Force" in cases of self-defence. Remember, ignorance does not equate with innocence.

FORTRESS STORMING

Acknowledgements:
Everyone we meet adds to our perception of the world around us;
everyone we meet adds to our understanding of the Martial Arts.
Special thanks must go to our Instructors over the years,
including (in chronological order)
our parents,
Peter Maduro, Jim Harvey, Yoshinobu Ohta, Keinosuke Enoeda,
Phil Trebilcock, George Dillman, Leon Jay,
Patrick McCarthy, Russell Stutely, Rick Moneymaker, Anthony Blades,
Peter Holmes, Eddie Stokes, Tom Muncy, Ron Van Browning,
Martyn Harris, Neil Ellison & Stuart Howe.

Special Thanks: The martial artists who appear in this guide are students and helpers at Eikoku Karate-do Kei-kokai. They did not ask to appear in here, but were prepared to pose at great risk to their self-esteem. *Mike Daniels, Rod Kingman, Sonja Halcro, Mark Archer, Dave Floyd, Thank You.*

Table of Contents

Foreword

By Russell Stutely

I have known John Burke for about 9 years now, and have seen him grow from a 1st kyu in Shotokan to one of the most knowledgeable and able Kata Bunkai experts in the UK. John has moved rapidly through the ranks due to his uncanny ability to absorb knowledge and information, and more importantly his ability to pass on that knowledge in a clear, precise, and easily understood manner. Essentially the quiet, unassuming man of the Karate world, it is time for this eloquent and engaging Karate-ka to break out, so to speak, and show the Shotokan World what they have been missing.

John is highly intelligent, thought provoking, easy going, yet extremely serious student of the Arts. He is continually looking at new ideas and innovations to pass on to his ever growing family of students. I am proud to say that over the years, not only has John been a fantastic student of mine, but he has become a friend also.

His latest work on the kata Bassai, a full 200 page book is both absorbing intellectually for the very experienced Kata Bunkai Karate-ka and exciting to those Martial Artists that are looking for the "light at the end of the tunnel".

I can pay this work no higher compliment than to place it at the very top of my list of recommended products.

Keep up the great work, John

Russell Stutely
Summer 2004, Cyprus
Russell Stutely is a Renshi,
co-founder of the Open Circle Institute (international martial arts governing body),
founder of the Open Circle Fighting Method,
and holds Dan grades in Shotokan Karate,
Torite Jutsu,
Okinawan Kempo,
Kickboxing,
and Kung Fu.

What is this book about?

This book is about mythology. It is about asking questions and taking responsibility for what we believe. It is about testing the dogma that is spouted without research by so many martial arts instructors today.

There's nothing wrong with taking advice, but one must make sure that the advice is being given for the right reasons, by someone who might know the answers. When it comes to martial arts there are many different approaches to training and teaching, and no single, all-powerful, over-lord to say who is doing it right and who is doing it wrong. The answers of one teacher are right from their point of view or they wouldn't be giving those answers. The problem comes from the answers being given having little or nothing to do with the question being asked. Parallel lines of training cannot be understood when the end results are not in harmony.

That is to say; everyone learning martial arts needs a teacher to correct them. What you have to check is that your instructor can direct you where you want to go. The best sports instructor may (or may not) be a great self defence instructor. The opposite is also possible. If your chosen path is a sporting path then the sports instructor will take you right to your destination. The same sports karate instructor might be able to help if you need or want self defence techniques, but if you spend every lesson doing sports karate then you will get very good at doing sports karate but not very good at doing self defence. If your instructor is not working towards the same goals as you are you might wish to change instructors.

Every student should question where their lessons are leading them. If you take that message on board and question what the author has written here then he cannot be angry about it. Any teacher should be pleased by their students or fellow researchers testing the validity of their claims. Too often the position of a martial arts instructor, accompanied by terms like *sensei* or master lead to ego related posturing that prevents the freedom to research and develop technique that works for the individual student. It becomes a case of "Do as I say", with the reason for doing so being "Because I say so".

There has been much rubbish spouted about the martial arts over the years. Some of it is well-meant but mistaken, some of it is simple repetition of accepted but unacceptable dogma; and some of it will get you injured.

Now, everyone is entitled to their opinion, and there are many people who do not agree with the author, just as there are many who do. Most of us, reasonable and intelligent people, will realise that every argument has it's flaws, and that every "fact" has a disputable basis. The rantings in this book are directed at those who do not question, or will not question, the teachings of those who have gone before.

Some martial arts instructors have created ivory towers for themselves, believing only their own press, no longer researching (some not even training). They get more grades and higher grades, and accolades for all they have "accomplished". These instructors create associations which barricade them from anyone outside who might question their judgement, and anyone from within who questions them is usually expelled. Within their fortresses they feel safe; so here we go—fortress storming.

Will this book change the way the world of Martial arts revolves? Not at all. ...But if... If we can keep people questioning their practice and their aims, and whether their instructors are teaching to the same ends... then maybe there will be more *study* of martial arts and less repetition for the sake of covering up an instructor's inability to teach applications.

This book is about one Karate Kata, and, for those who can see it, about all Karate Kata.

This book grew out of the outrage shown by one of my students—"They can't write that!" she said. She had been a studious learner, constantly looking for more information on her chosen art. She would buy Karate books. Proudly, she would bring me her purchases, and yet she would wonder why the people in the books were doing applications to their kata that clearly did not work. "Someone should write what works." Some people *have* written what works, but just as there is room for more than one opinion so is there room for more than one book on Karate technique.

I hope this book does it for you.

Before setting out on this project, I spent some time considering whether to include the barbaric applications that we know Bassai Dai to include. I wrestled with the moral dilemma of whether it was right to potentially show people that I had never met such gruesome techniques. The Karate teacher has a duty to pass on quality information to quality students. There might be unscrupulous individuals who would buy the book and could mis-use the information.

In the end I came to the conclusion that only dedicated Karate-ka would take the time to read the things I was writing, and only dedicated Karate-ka would practice often and well enough to make use of the information. There are easier ways to hurt people, after all.

I trust that dedicated Karate-ka spend enough time wrestling with the morality of their training and it's implications to know what is right.

What is Karate?

Karate is an art, properly named **Karate-Do**. This is Japanese for "*The Way of the Empty Hand*". It is usually taught as a method of punching, blocking, kicking and striking, but as I will show in the following pages, it also includes joint-locks, strangulations, grappling, and throws.

Karate is commonly thought to have originated in Japan, specifically the island chain (the Ryukyu islands) south of Kyushu, Japan. It is the art's humble origin on Okinawa, the main part of the chain, that makes the history of Karate so fascinating—and explains why the things which are commonly mis-taught today are the way they are.

Okinawa was, and is, a great melting pot of cultures. It takes on characteristics from Japan, but also from China and Taiwan. It was a centre of trade with China at a time when the Japanese would not openly admit to trading with China. Okinawa was never a rich country as it has, at times, paid tribute (tax) to both of it's parent nations. It also had various bans put in place against the nobility carrying weapons (firstly in order to stop them warring amongst themselves, later to stop them resisting the Japanese). In this climate Karate was developed, not by peasants, but by the noble classes looking to continue to defend themselves.

Kara Te Do

The writing used for Kara Te Do currently depicts the ideas of "emptiness" or the "void", "Hand", and "The Way".

The last of these is the same character you find in Taoism. The first of them is a recent replacement (less than a hundred years) for the character depicting a link to the Tang dynasty of China.

The older reading would have been "China Hand". The reason for the change can be found in the fledgling organisation of the art into something popular enough for spreading to the Japanese mainland. To fit in with Japanese ideals and to avoid anti-Chinese sentiment in pre-WWII Japan, basically, to gain acceptance,-a very important thing in many societies—it was felt that the art should take on certain Japanese characteristics.

It was to gain acceptance that Karate teachers adopted the use of uniforms (do-gi); it was to gain acceptance that a competitive format was adopted; and a ranking structure using coloured belts. It might also have been the only reason that Karate survived World War II's anti-militarism ban on warrior activities.

The governing body which laid these structures down for Karate was the Dai Nippon Butokukai. Following WWII that organisation was officially dissolved, as were any other activities that occupying American forces thought promoted Japanese militarism. Because Karate was not organised to a high degree the DNBK was not able to homogenise it, and so today we have many different styles, and many different "masters".

Today, Karate can be many things, it can be whatever you want it to be.

It is a **Sport**, teaching competitors to push themselves to athletic heights and monumental efforts of perseverance.

It is a **Spiritual Discipline**, an austere method of introspective discovery. It has been labelled as "moving zen", and it has just as many paradoxical foundations as zen.

It is a **Fighting Method**, using an economy of motion and generation of force second to none.

It is an interesting **Hobby**, a method of losing weight that does not rely upon the use of expensive equipment or changes to the diet (although that can help).

It is a **business**, an educational system to improve the quality of our society.

This art, then, is a cipher—becoming different things to different people. There are as many different perceptions of what the art is as there are practitioners and observers.

Practice usually consists of the repeated performance of the *three K*s. *Kihon*— the practice of basic/fundamental techniques. *Kata*—formal exercises. And *Kumite*—the set sparring and later, free sparring.

What your basics, kata, and kumite practice consist of will depend to a large extent on your instructor. For some, realism is not an issue, it is all about the act of practising; for others it is all about sport; for others, all about self defence. For most instructors there is some kind of mix, and I believe that most misunderstandings about our arts occur when one element is mistaken for another.

One's development in this art is plotted through a series of ranks of increasing difficulty. Most aspire towards Black Belt, yet experienced practitioners know that this is only the first level of real attainment; the end of being a beginner.

You can't compare ranks of people from different schools; their methodology, training style, and requirements might be quite different. The only people for whom a belt has any real meaning are the person who earned it (they know what it's worth), and the person who awarded it (they know the standard that they place on it). Usually those within an association or organisation will also appreciate the award, but not always—this is a personal journey, not a competition.

Just to make it really clear, let's say outright: Black Belt does not confer mastery. Having a black belt does not make one proficient in all aspects of their art. Pick who you follow carefully.

Do vs Jutsu

Karate-do = The Way of the Empty Hand. Karate-jutsu = Empty Hand Skills.

Many martial artists spend their time arguing the pro's and cons of Do and Jutsu, whether the Karate they practice is an Art or a Science. They seem to find merit in the argument that a "Way" cannot be as strong as a "Skill". The argument usually rests on the fact that most *do* arts have become sports or are heavily influenced by the requirements of the sporting part of their art. This, then, comes to mean that if you are performing a *do* you are performing for sport. By definition, this is not true. A *do*/way is always about what one must go through for ones' self; not in competition with others (the definition for sport).

Apart from any balance found in practising something spiritual, we would argue that you can pursue a strong, defensively violent set of skills as a Way. The two terms are not mutually exclusive.

There was a Japanese teacher who taught hard classes, the kind with blood and sweat in equal measure. One of his students asked if this was because he believed in the "jutsu" end of Karate. He replied that there was too much practice of mere *jutsu*, and that he was creating a school which really followed the *Do*.

I believe that what the teacher meant was that too many people, even those interested in the use of force, self defence, etc., only practice technique—jutsu; skills—without the practice of readying the mind and spirit for those and other situations.

If you make practice a way of life, preferably towards a refined goal, then you are practising a **do**, not just a *jutsu*.

What is Kata?

- A routine, a set of movements,
- A formal exercise.
- A testing/examination requirement.
- A method of moving meditation.

What kata is **not** is an imaginary fight dealing with multiple opponents. One only has to apply common sense to see the outcome of trying to do your kata on a gang of 8 or 18 attackers. While you are dealing with number 1 the others have rearranged your ideals.

Kata is taught in many Karate schools around the world as "something you have to learn" in order to get your next grade. It is explained with poor applications if any are given at all. In many schools they trot out dogma like "when you are a higher grade you will understand" - yet there is always a higher grade to become. In some schools they simply do not bother explaining their kata.

In the following pages we take one kata, a kata which is important to many Karate -ka, and show How to do it, What it doesn't do (as shown in numerous classes around the world), and What it can do.

We urge all martial artists to practice these moves with caution. They are danger-ous! That is your clue to why they are not often taught.

How to...

Introduction to Bassai Dai
Origins of Bassai Dai
What is Kata?
How to...
Performance of Kata

Bassai

The purpose of this book is to remind practitioners of the Bassai kata and how to get the best from the techniques that make the kata whole.

No publication can *teach* a kata and its applications; this can only be done by a qualified instructor in a time set aside for tuition. You need real instruction, but deciding who is qualified to teach can sometimes be difficult, especially as first impressions generally only show you who can yell the most or who has a "fun" class. We *can* help to jog the memory and provide inspiration for further study of one of the greatest exercises in karate.

The Bassai kata is one of the most prevalent in martial arts. It occurs in many different styles with only slight differences. This in itself shows a common root to the traditions which share Bassai. Known variously as Patsai, Passai, Bassai Dai, or other variations, this kata can be seen in Taekwondo, Shito Ryu, Goju Ryu, Kyokushinkai, Wado Ryu, and many other styles of karate. Different *Sokes* have placed the emphasis on different techniques, but truthfully, they are all Bassai.

The version shown within heralds from Shotokan, nominally the style of Funakoshi Gichin, credited by many as the *father of modern karate-do.*

The Shotokan was the first purpose-built karate dojo in Japan. The style is hugely popular, making it quite common. It was due to the efforts of Funakoshi's students in taking Shotokan across the world that Karate as a whole is as popular as it is today. Without the distribution of Shotokan, Karate might not have survived into the modern age.

Much Shotokan practice is based around competition karate. This means that many of the movements are only used if they are useful for scoring points, neglecting techniques which would get you banned from competition (but might save your life).

Certainly, many movements within Shotokan have become homogenised and made safe for practice by school children. This does not mean that the old, dangerous techniques are removed, just that their applications have merely been overlooked in favour of simplistic explanations and hidden by the aesthetic required for competition.

The writing shown here is the Kanji for Bassai Dai.

Originally it would have been written differently, but Funakoshi chose to write it in Japanese (which was a foreign language to him). It must be understood that the Kanji are not words, but rather ideas. They are pictograms conveying images and suggestions to the eye, and without context they are meaningless.

The term is made up of three characters:

the last one is **Dai**, meaning the greater part, *major* (as opposed to minor), or great (as in Great Britain).

The first character is **Batsu**, meaning to *extract* or remove.

The second character is **Sai** which is usually translated as Fortress but more likely means *obstacle* or blockage.

The usual given translation in the west is "**To Storm a Fortress, Major Version**".

We might think of it more literally as "*the major way of removing obstacles*".

Bassai Dai, written with
Japanese Calligraphy

Origins

Bassai itself is alleged to have been in use at the time of **Bushi Matsumura Sokon** (1797/1809—1901?: an exact date cannot be supplied as there are some discrepancies). Matsumura was trained by **Todi** (Karate) **Sakugawa**, who trained under **Takahara Peichin** (1683—1760) and Chinese Envoy **Kung Shang K'ung** (Kosukun—the source of the Kanku Dai kata of modern Shotokan) in 1756. Whether Sakugawa or his teachers knew the Bassai formal exercise is unknown, but we can see that Bassai has been around for something like 200 years! Matsumura is known to have influenced the martial artists of the towns of Shuri and Tomari in Okinawa, leading to this form being handed down in many different karate lineages.

The Mandarin Chinese term *"Baoshi"*, the Fuzhou dialect term *"Baassai"*, and the Quanzhou dialect term *"Pausai"* relate to the characters for "Leopard-Lion", which may be an indication of the kata's origins in Leopard boxing and Lion boxing forms of kung-fu. This information comes from Okinawan karate researcher **Kinjo Akio** (via **Joe Swift** and the **IRKRS**). Similarly, **Murakami Katsumi** refers to parts of the kata as reminding him of the *Wuxing Quan* (5 Element Fist) form of *Xingyi Quan*.

When trying to find the "oldest" or "first" Bassai we must not overlook the possibility that some practitioner of old named the form after someone or the techniques of someone who was their senior or mentor in order to give the kata "validity". This makes the form appear older that it may actually be, and does not necessarily mean that the most ancient stylist actually practised the form.

The other consideration is that the kata consists of moves which have been practised long before they were organised into a set mnemonic called Bassai, and as such the knowledge contained may actually be a lot older than the form suggests.

Remember that as an island art, Karate was practised by few of the Okinawan people, and that until it was carried over to Japan there was little in the way of "standardisation of practice", as each new generation of Karate-ka would make alterations and variations for their own body-type or to suit the needs of their students. After all, without a grading system or syllabus, there was no need for one man's kata to look the same as the next man's kata - just that the principles be passed on correctly from one generation to the next.

What is Kata?- A more detailed answer.

More important than which version is shown here are the **principles** espoused, which are universal. They are common to martial arts the world over.

The kata exists as a means of recording the favoured techniques of a particular teacher; and as such is a living document which is highly biased towards the times and place of its origination and any subsequent adaptation.

Kata = style

This is why there were originally different kata—to show how different teachers would have their techniques and art preserved. The kata (the plural of a kata is several "kata") act as memory aids for students who cannot be with their teacher every day for private practice, and also present a means of performing movements strongly which would otherwise damage a training partner should they receive the unbridled technique.

Developed in a time and place under occupation of foreign forces, Karate was practiced in secret. Karate was practised in private houses and gardens by enthusiasts in small numbers for self protection. This meant that there were very few books on the art, and many of the documents which did exist were subsequently destroyed during the bombing of Okinawa during World War II. Kata were the memory aid for the students of those times, the living books to preserve the teachings of the masters.

Kata = form

Kata had purpose, they were not the reason for training, but rather the culmination of it!

Nowadays there is an unfortunate trend towards the use of kata as a standard of performance for the awarding of grade (without any real understanding of the subject matter), and the aesthetic perfection of movement for the use in competition (judged without understanding the movements). New kata are even being created based on how they are used to win competitions!

There are two sets of kanji currently used to write the word "kata". One is immoveable and engraved in stone, the other allows for interpretation. Which does your group use?

How To...

In the following pages we will show the shapes that are made during the kata, and provide details of what the techniques can be used for. There is also a section showing what the kata does not do, just to dispel the myths.

When performing kata there are many elements to consider.
The Mindset of the practitioner must demonstrate
readiness: the concentration of the mind upon what the body is doing - a feeling of imminent explosion of technique;
zanshin: constant awareness of surroundings and actions.

The Body of the performer must demonstrate

balance - not just of weight, but of hard ness and softness;
correct **timing** - including which parts are performed slowly and which parts have an extra burst of speed;
expansion and contraction of the body - many moves do not just move the hands and feet but integrate the whole;
correct **breathing**;
use of **kiai**.

This is all in addition to learning the shapes and directions of the kata.

The process of taking a kata apart is known as *Bunkai*. There are many levels of bunkai, from the simplistic, used to develop the look and feel of a kata; to the secret *Okuden* level of meaning, to be discovered by the most dedicated of students.

Some conventions which occur within should be explained for clarity. Where we use the term Embusen, we are referring to the main line of the kata. Although the term may properly be used for the entire shape drawn out with the feet, we choose to mean only the most significant line of the form.

The term "he" when referring to an attacker is not meant to be sexist or imply that the techniques are only usable against a male. Neither is the term "he" meant to imply that only males can use the techniques herein when referring to a defender. Statistically, most attacks are perpetrated by males and most martial artists are males; this does not have any negative connotation for females. These are purely terms of convenience to make the document easier to read and the subject matter more approachable.

The same can be said for our use of the phrase "martial artist" throughout this work. There are many who would argue the semantics that Karate and the associated disciplines were never used in the field of war and have no right to the term martial (derived from Mars, God of War) and for the most part are not even artistic (many lack the freedom to express themselves through their actions and as no creation takes place there is no art). This kind of petty bickering has been ignored in favour of a commonly used term to prevent having to explain "combative discipline" or "fighting art" or any of the other homonyms which could potentially be used.

Similarly, although applications may not be used "to block" they may still be referred to by the common (mis-)translation of "block" when the term **uke** really means "to receive".

Perhaps one of the most important translation issues in this work is the term **Bunkai**. The term literally means "to take apart and understand". This is what this work is about. If you were actually to use any of the techniques then that would be **Oyo**: "to respond/react with use". The difference is that bunkai is an academic or abstract/theoretical exercise, whilst oyo is the application in the circumstances which require it.

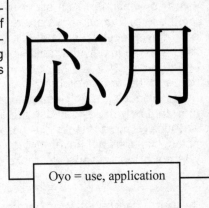

分解

Bunkai = analysis

The bunkai herein are effective fight stopping techniques. They are not the <u>only</u> ones for each movement, and there may be easier or harder variations available. Space does not permit the inclusion of "every" application available. Variations can always be found working with one of our instructors, attending an organised Seminar (which we conduct regularly), or watching the Martial Arts Technical Series video of this kata.

応用

Oyo = use, application

PERFORMANCE by Mike Daniels, Nidan

BASSAI DAI
To Storm a Fortress - Major

There is a Minor version of this kata which it is believed was created by **Itosu Anko**.

The prevalent feeling of this kata is of surging forward, a symbol of karate's **indomitable spirit**. There is a good mix of slow and fast movements, and deliberate turns with precise applications.

This form is often used by students all the way to Shodan, such is the importance, elegance, and power of it. Such a kata needs *study*. Anything less is superficial and will not make one into a good karate-ka.

1) From a ready position. Bring the feet together, bow, name the kata.

2) Place the right fist in front of the dantien at 45 degrees from the body and cup the right fist with the left hand. (Yoi.) The elbows are relaxed, the shoulders pulled down and back. It is important to tuck the coccyx bone in, tilting the hips slightly and keeping the spine upright. The head feels like it is suspended by a wire from the ceiling. Do not begin the kata with a feeling of heaviness in the skull.

3) Pull the fist sharply back to the left hip by folding the left elbow. At the same time raise the right knee. Do not dip the chin, but rather tilt the pelvic plate. There is a feeling of coiling ready for an imminent explosion of power.

4) Step quickly forward into kosadachi, making morote Uchikomi. The right fist should end no higher than the shoulder. The feeling should be one of rolling the arms around to the front. This particularly devastating move throws all of the weight forwards. The effort should be palpable. The "supporting" hand is open, the wrist straight.

Do not move on to the next section immediately, but rather take a second to focus, balance, and then begin the next set of movements.

4.

5

5a

5-6) Move the left foot backwards until a comfortable mawate can be performed, make uchiuke with the right arm while facing the rear in left zenkutsudachi.

Follow immediately with left gyaku uchiuke without altering the stance. Full use of hip means that on the second movement the right hip will come forward of shomen.

Be careful to keep the left knee still whilst performing this move.

6

6a.

7-8) Look over the right shoulder. Make mawate into right zenkutsudachi facing the front with left gyaku-sotouke. Follow immediately with right uchiuke.

Please note that these movements require *two* arms to effect correctly. On the uchiuke there is a characteristic "tearing" sound as the elbows pass.

9) Look to the right. Pull the right foot back, drop the weight while keeping the spine vertical, bending from the knees. The right arm makes sukuiuke.

Turn to the right. The feeling should be of a strong pull from the hips.

10) Step out to the right into right zenkutsudachi, making sotouke just using the right arm. The left hand remains on the hip.

11) Immediately follow with left gyaku-uchiuke. Again note the use of hips in the movement.

12) Pull the left foot up to face the front in uchihachijidachi, the right fist makes hikite at the right hip, the left vertical fist sits on top.

13) Push the left hand out to the front making tate shutouchi.

Habitually, there is a slight rising of the open hand to the level of the shoulder before slowly pushing the hand out. The palm turns from facing the shoulder to facing away from it.

14)   Make left hikite and right chudanzuki/chokuzuki

15)   The right fist comes back to the left pectoral muscle, the thumb barely touching, then makes gyaku-uchiuke.

Turn the left toes out to the left pivoting on the left heel, turn the right heel out to the right, pivoting on the ball of the foot into a shortened left zenkutsudachi. The feeling should be of a strong counter-winding of the hip to the action of the arm.

16)   Punch chudanzuki to the front with the left fist, reversing the previous stance change back to face the front in uchihachijidachi, the right fist makes hikite at the right hip.

17-18) Turn the right toes out to the right pivoting on the right heel, turn the left heel out to the left, pivoting on the ball of the foot into a shortened right zenkutsudachi. The left fist comes back to the right pectoral muscle and then makes gyaku-uchiuke to the front.

19) Step past the left hand along the embusen into a right kokutsudachi, making shutouke.

Note that the feet and knees pass in stepping through, don't be tempted to "thud" forward, but place the toes before the heel and use the front foot as a "brake". There should not be any bounce from the front leg onto the back leg, but rather a feeling of precise placement.

20) Step forwards into left kokutsudachi making shutouke.

21) Step forwards into right kokutsudachi making shutouke.

22) Step backwards into left kokutsudachi making shutouke. A common question is "How soon after stepping forward should one step back for this movement?" A senior karate-ka once told this author that there is no point in stepping backwards until one is balanced and firmly located forwards; in other words, step back don't bounce back.

23-24) Twist the torso to shomen, shifting the weight forward into a shortened zenkutsudachi. At the same time pass the right hand beneath the left elbow and up in a slow circular motion, the hip becoming gyaku hanmi. The right hand descends until the fingers are at shoulder height, the arms and hip feel coiled.

It is vital that the head does not turn as the body twists. There is a strong feeling of torsion in the hips/pelvis as this move is conducted, making the body coiled and ready for the next technique. Both hands rest in the "tiger-mouth" shape.

25-26) Raise the right knee between the arms and kick kansetsugeri to the front, dragging the hands up to just below the right nipple and make fists. **KIAI.** The palms of the fists are towards the floor.

This is a key moment in the kata, and all too often subject to sloppy recovery of the leg and little or no preparedness for the next movement.

26a Side View   27.   27   28.

27) Look behind, along the embusen, recover the knee and step down into left kokutsudachi facing the rear. Make shutouke.

28) Step forwards into right kokutsudachi make shutouke.

29.   29a.   29b.   29c.

29) Pull the right foot back so that the feet are together, keep the spine vertical whilst the knees are bent.

Curl the hands, as fists, back to the dantien and roll them vertically just in front of the body. When the fists are just above the head, palms forwards, they have just two knuckles from each hand touching. This sequence is conducted purposefully but not overly slowly.

The push upwards with the knees should finish at the same time as the fists reach their uppermost point.

30-31) Pull the fists apart abruptly, then circle them forwards and down to make a left hand and right hand tetsui strike to the ribs simultaneously. At the same time step out into right zenkutsudachi.

Avoid the feeling of falling forwards, and instead cultivate the spirit of pushing forwards with strong intention.

32) Shift both feet without changing stance or height to punch right chudanzuki.

Do not pull the hands back to the hip prior to punching, but commit suddenly, directly from the tetsui. Beware of shrugging the shoulders in the middle of this move, instead concentrate on keeping low and thrusting "from the floor". A good zenkutsudachi will never totally lock the back knee out despite appearing straight, so pushing forward is still possible.

33) Look over the left shoulder. Shift the left foot across, cutting downwards with the left hand (little finger uppermost) and parrying with the right hand just in front of the forehead.

34) Complete the mawate by thrusting the right hand down, palm upwards, whilst pulling the left open hand up with the palm towards the right ear. Note that the elbows come together.

35) Slowly pull the left foot back to the right making manji-gamae. Hands and feet finish their movements simultaneously.

The manji-gamae has one arm dropped down to the level of gedan barai and the other arm has a vertical forearm in line with the head and the elbow held at shoulder height. It may help to imagine a line between the uppermost fist, the eyes, and the lowermost fist. The fundamental issue is to make sure that the fists are aligned, the shoulder-blades must be squeezed together or the rear hand will naturally sit forward.

36-37) Moving anti-clockwise step fumikomi towards the front and land in kibadachi making right gedan barai. Think of the left arm as being an aiming arm that the right arm travels along.

Once again the foot and fist must land at the same time. The right hand comes down <u>over</u> the head for the smallest circle. It is too easy for practitioners to make exaggerated circular movements—this is just laziness.

38-39) Look to the left, towards the rear of the embusen. Cross the arms, grabbing over the top with the right, placing the left horizontal hand below the right armpit. Both hands are palm downwards, right hand open, left hand closed.

Slowly make right hikite, expanding the chest and at the last moment turn the left hand to a vertical position. Ensure that the right elbow is "pinched" against your side, not allowed to roam.

40) Use the right foot to make mikazukigeri towards the left hand. Do not drop the hand, nor turn the body too soon. Ensure that the palm is contacted by the sole of the foot, not the edge.

41) Step down into kibadachi and make mawashi-empi uchi. The right fist is palm down.

42) Remaining in the stance, drop the right fist down, keeping the left fist against the right bicep.

43-44) Quickly drop the left fist down and bring the right fist back up to the left bicep, then drop the right fist down, replacing the left fist against the right bicep. There is a noticeable and distinct rhythm to this set of three movements where the second and third strikes follow each other quickly (half-breaths) whilst the first one has a "count" (breath) of its own.

45) Look to the rear of the embusen over the right shoulder. Move the right foot to make right zenkutsudachi facing the rear. Make left hikite and place the right fist vertically on the left fist. The left foot must pivot in order to make the stance correct, but there is no need to shift it in any direction.

46) Make yamazuki, left fist uppermost. The spine is in line with the angle of the rear leg, showing the head forwards of the hips for one of the few times in kata. The lower arm is nearly horizontal, slightly aiming up. The upper arm is slightly aiming down, but nearly horizontal. The upper arm looks similar to ageuke, but has not finished twisting or making the correct angle. The idea is that lines drawn from each fist would meet at some point in the distance. They are in line one above the other, and neither fist is to the fore of the other.

47.   47a.   48.

48a.   48b

47) Pull the right foot back to place the feet together. Straighten the knees at the end of the movement. Make right hikite with the left fist vertically above. The move is not slow, but neither is it performed as vigorously as the forward motions.

There should be a strong feeling of winding up the hips, setting the tone and intention for the performance of this key characteristic of the kata. The breath is drawn in throughout the movement and held for a fraction of a second before the correct exhalation during the next movement. The best practitioners generate a feeling of "impending action" at this stage.

48) Raise the left knee quickly and step forwards into left zenkutsudachi, making yamazuki, right fist uppermost.

Be careful not to step out diagonally, the movement is directly forwards, and the stance may be somewhat narrower than that taught at beginner's levels. Create a feeling of this kata's name.

49.   49a   50.

50a.   50

49) Pull the left foot back to place the feet together. Make left hikite with the right fist vertically above.

50) Raise the right knee quickly and step forwards into right zenkutsudachi, making yamazuki, left fist uppermost.

This whole sequence usually defines the kata. Much study and practice of this section is suggested.

Do not rush, develop the feeling of gathering your forces and storming forwards, returning like a wave withdrawing from the shore and, just as surely as the wave, crashing again upon the defences of the imaginary opponent (and demolishing them).

51-53) Look over the right shoulder. Move the left foot out to the right, pivoting on the right foot. The right fist punches up in the air as the left fist makes hikite.

The right forearm swings in front of the body as a long, low left zenkutsudachi is made out to the side at 90 degrees to the previous direction of travel. The nagashi uke then pulls sharply back and aims to the front, horizontally with the palm up, similar to a descending uraken.

The hips are shomen to the left, the right elbow tight to the hip at the end of the movement. The feeling throughout this movement is of a whip flowing quickly and then cracking back (with kime). The right fist travels the longest route, with the elbow remaining relatively close to the body, far less distance travelled.

Avoid the tendency to look down at the fist, but instead concentrate the eyes towards the front of the embusen.

54-56) Punch upwards with the left fist as the hips begin to twist.

Mawate to face to the right, making a long, low right zenkutsudachi, the right fist makes hikite. The forearm sweeps in front of the body then pulls back sharply and aims to the front, horizontally with the palm up. The hips are shomen to the right, the left elbow tight to the hip.

This reversal of the last sequence has the same character about it. Keep the eyes to the front throughout the movement.

As with most movements in Karate, the whole of this sequence is generated from the hips. When we us our "whip" analogy we must be aware of the *whip's handle* which is the original generator of the whip's power - that being your hip; and the intention of the movement (the arm holding the handle). Without these the movement relies upon wooden arm movements.

57) Look across 45 degrees to the right.

Bring the left foot up to the right, preparing the armsfor shuto uke with the elbows together.

Step forwards at 45 degrees into right kokutsudachi and make shutouke.

58) Deliberately look to the left, at a 45 degree angle to the embusen.

59) Slowly twist the position so that the kokutsudachi and shutouke move through ninety degrees without changing.

Effectively, making shutouke in kokutsudachi at a "north-west" 45 degree angle, one appears to be looking the wrong way (to the "south-east").

This movement should be a gathering of forces for one last strike, winding up the hips, inhaling, and preparing the mind.

60-61) Move the right foot up to the left while preparing the arms and then step out at 45 degrees to the embusen into left kokutsudachi and make shutouke. **KIAI**.

This final burst of technique should have every last ounce of your energy involved in it. It is too easy to have performed the "difficult parts" of the kata and then "relax" the last section because it has a slow part or because the end of the performance is in sight. The idea must be to remain aware of your surroundings and the intention and feeling of the form until the very last - every time it is performed!

62) Pull the left foot back to the right, the right fist in front of the dantien, cup it with the left hand.

The pull backwards is performed with great control. There is no need to rock forwards before pulling back; the front knee is already a little bent so it is possible to push the ball of the foot against the floor in order to move backwards.

Place the hands by the sides. Bow.

Make a ready position.

Remember to finish each performance with dignity and remaining awareness, controlling the breathing and focus of the eyes.

Real Kata Bunkai

APPLICATIONS

The kata shown on the preceding pages may be a requirement for grading in many styles of Karate, but those who are really interested in their art should also know what the moves mean. Without application the kata remains a dance. With application we preserve the original meaning of Karate as a method of self protection. This can only be true if the applications are meaningful to the people who preserve them.

There are only so many ways to move the arms and legs in self protection, yet some ways are clearly advantageous - just as some ways will lead to an even greater problem. Our job, then, is to find applications which make sense, and which can be used with various levels of force to achieve various desirable results.

Rarely is anything in this world *original*. Much research has been conducted into this kata and its applications, but some of the breakthroughs have come from non -karate-ka.

Attending seminars with martial artists from different styles, the author has sometimes been shocked to be told that "*this is an aikido move*" when he clearly recognised that the move performed without a partner would be the solo template in a karate kata. Talking with ju-jutsu-ka one is often presented with techniques which just scream out to you that if they were performed without a partner would be exactly the moves of kata. Certain Kung Fu practitioners may mock the rigid forms of karate, but the kata moves are only exaggerations of the same principles that they work with.

These applications to the techniques from Bassai Dai *work*. They have been experimented with and used by small ladies and big men. Housewives, door staff, members of the constabulary and security services have all been able to make practical use of the technique applications which follow this section. Thankfully, some of the nastier applications have remained theoretical - but the principle can be shown to be effective in even a restrained manner - so the end result of a lack of control, or a deliberate use of force, can be extrapolated.

Common themes in our applications include:

- Beginning at a range where there is a real danger of being struck by any of the attacker's weapons.
- Only using common methods of attack which an untrained attacker might reasonably be expected to use.
- Beginning at a casual guarded position rather than "in a stance".
- Making both hands work together—never leaving one hand "ready" or

"pulling back to make the other hand more powerful".

- Making contact with the attacker half-way through the technique—not at the end.
- Penetration with each technique, not just surface contact.
- Leaving no gap between the attacker and our own body when seeking to control them.
- Co-ordination of Mind, Breath, and Body.

When analysing the pattern of attacks which occur "in the street" we see that there will usually be a pre-amble/"interview"/set-up/distraction which is verbal. The trained martial artist must recognise these factors and use it to raise his energy level from casual to "primed for action". This does not mean jump in to a full zenkutsudachi. Being ready is a state of mind—preparedness.

Common types of attack (which Patrick McCarthy Hanshi refers to as the **Habitual Acts of Physical Violence**) might include:

- Hook **punches**, straight punches, upper-cuts
- Single wrist **grab**, cross-body wrist grab, double wrist grab
- Grab at the forearm, elbow, or shoulder; either one-handed or two-handed
- **Pushing**, single-handed or two-handed from the front, side, or rear.
- Bear-hug grabs from the front, side, or rear
- Strangulations/neck-grabs; one-handed, two-handed, from the front, side, or rear
- Grabbing the groin.
- Head-**locks**; facing forwards or backwards
- Full-Nelson or half-Nelson locks from the rear, or Rugby tackle rushes from the front or side.
- Head-butt.
- Back-handed strikes, slaps
- Descending strikes or slaps
- **Kicks** to the shin or thigh
- Knee to the groin

The many variations on the above which may come from types of clothing or situation might also be investigated, but recognise the core principle: an assault is when one of the above methods enters within your personal space.

Recognise the attack's imminence and prepare to react to it. Know the effects of adrenaline and how they manifest. Have your plan ready and be prepared to see it through. As explained in the previous section; strikes from behind can only be deflected if you are psychic or there is some kind of warning (shadow/reflection/verbal abuse, etc.). If you manage to turn then it is no longer an attack from the rear.

Detractors may say that the combinations shown are flights of fancy; that the simplest solutions are better: "Just hit them". It is true that simple is good, and that pre-emptive striking is the only *sure* way of "getting your shot in". You will see that many of our applications do involve hitting the opponent. We use the kata applications to show different circumstances and different ways of "just hitting them". With kata as a training method these techniques become the programmed subconscious automatic responses to violent stimuli.

The key here is that these techniques belong to the world of "what we might do once the attack has begun". The emphasis of each technique and combination is to put the defender in a better position than they started in - if pummelling an attacker is your solution then you should do it from a position where you cannot be struck again/back at so easily. If your chosen method of self-protection involves restraining an assailant then you should be able to do it from a safe position or it will not last long.

Secondly, many people wish to apprehend, restrain, or subdue an attacker rather than destroy them. This is a matter of choice and many of the kata movements can be "toned down" to allow restraint—it's hard to tone down a punch.

We must state once again that just because the techniques shown are *able* to be used does not mean that you *should* use them. Nor does it mean that we condone their use in the way they are shown, we merely present them as an alternative to "the usual suspects". When pulling apart kata (the science of bunkai) you don't actually *have to* hurt people. Just understand that the moves of the kata *could* hurt people, and that this is what they were designed for. You still have **free will**.

Context will always be the deciding factor in whether a technique and it's effects are justified, and this is another reason why books and videos merely serve to _remind_; not to *teach* techniques and how they should be applied.

Each of the techniques of Bassai manoeuvre the defender into a position where the anatomically weak areas become available to manipulate. This is a key to Bunkai. If important targets do not present themselves in an exposed/available condition then the bunkai is flawed. A punch in the shoulder blades will never be as good as a tap in the kidney area: if the shoulder blade is your only target then use it, but good bunkai will reveal kidneys, neck, or any of the other susceptible areas as targets.

In the following applications we choose to use the terminology of Oriental Medicine to describe the locations of the areas to be struck. We do this because:

i)   It was the science of the place and the times where the Art originated. Many practitioners continue to use the language and terminology of their Art's birthplace, so isn't it right that we should honour the tradition and practice by investigating the culture and values of the originators?

ii) Although there are Modern Western Medicine explanations for the results achieved they are more complicated to explain than "Fire Melts Metal". At our dojo we have a four page treatise on this very subject laminated to the wall, mostly using Latin medical terminology. Our students usually give up reading it on the second paragraph. It is easy to say that they should persevere (in order to understand), as they do with their physical training, yet there is descriptive analysis in the Traditional Oriental Medicine which is more readily available.

iii) The imagery conjured by 5 Element applications conveys better results than trying to strike nerves—call it mental conditioning if you will. Many people do not know what a nerve looks like nor the route it might take through the body, but the image of fire coursing along someone's arm is easily conjured.

iv) Students must study to understand. A kata should be the summation of knowledge, and those practising Bassai should have learned an awful lot. Of course they can study the western principles too, if they wish. This work is a reminder, but there is still more to explain.

A Quick Overview of Traditional Oriental Medicine

Traditional Oriental Medicine is based around observation of living creatures, unlike Modern Western medicine which is based on the study of dead things. Not mystical mumbo-jumbo as some have suggested, just a different "take" on the way things interact. We must remember that science is the result of a hypothesis (idea) which is observed to be true and tested enough times to be considered "fact". That these are different "facts" than are arrived at in Occidental medicine should not be considered proof that they are false, just that they are different— just as Tai Chi Chuan is different to Karate, the result still serves the same ends.

Oriental medicine formed around the conviction that an energy field exists within the body and around it which is dubbed **Ki** (also known as Chi/Qi/Prana). This energy is the life-force and it may be enhanced by certain exercises and manipulations. Acupuncture, acupressure, and reiki all revolve around the manipulation of Ki.

Yin-Yang

Any time there is a healing property there is also a *destructive* property. This is universally true, whether you are looking at western medicine or cookery; equal and opposite (**Inyo** in Japanese, Yin-Yang, more popularly, in Chinese). The destructive side of Eastern medicine is the use of fighting methods upon the body's Ki channels (**meridians**) through specific points on those channels (**pressure points**).

It seems to be that because chi/ki cannot be physically seen and its pathways do not appear as small tubes in the body that the Western scientist is dubious of its existence. Please remember that magnetic energy cannot be seen either, but a magnet placed on a sheet of paper covered in iron filings reveals the magnetic lines as the filings orient themselves to make the force's effect become visible— there just is no current correct medium to see the effect of ki in.

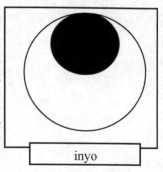

inyo

In these days of multiple new diseases and disruption to the natural order of the world more and more people, including scientists and doctors, are coming to the realisation that alternative methods of healing and the holistic worldview are of merit. So much of medicine is to do with treating symptoms and so little to do with curing the organism that there has to be a flaw in the logic of that system. It might be said that Oriental medicine treats *the person* and *their condition* and not

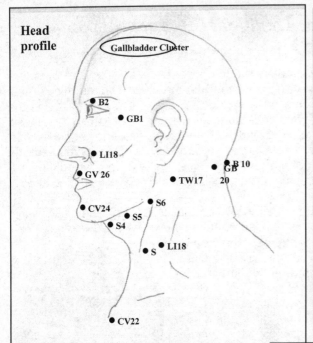

Head profile

Gallbladder Cluster

B2

GB1

LI18

GV 26

B 10
GB 20

TW17

CV24

S6

S5

S4

S

LI18

CV22

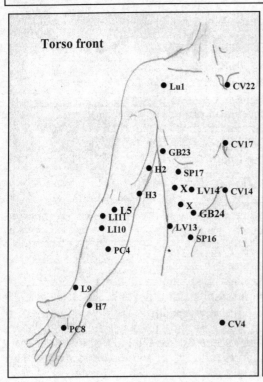

Torso front

Lu1

CV22

GB23

CV17

H2

SP17

H3

X   LV14   CV14

X

L5   GB24

LI11   LV13

LI10   SP16

PC4

L9

H7

PC8

CV4

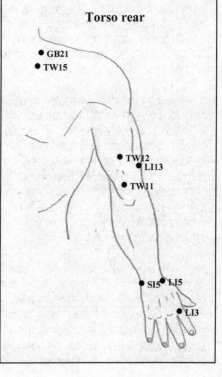

Torso rear

GB21

TW15

TW12

LI13

TW11

SI5   LI5

LI3

just the apparent effects.

The reverse of this, the martial arts, is also true. Techniques which effect the energetic system effect the *whole person* temporarily, not just their muscle or creating a black-eye, but instead creating a **Body Alarm Reaction**.

Some people claim that pressure points are too small to hit in a "real fight". We will show that if the correct applications are known and trained at the correct distance then it is actually difficult **to miss** pressure points in the techniques of Bassai. The problem with pressure points isn't hitting them; it's hitting them correctly! The techniques of the kata are designed to hit points in a sequence beneficial to the defender. The techniques of the kata are designed to show the correct angle and direction for an opponent to be struck on pressure points when the opponent is in a specific location.

More important is the idea that the techniques of the kata work just fine even if you know nothing about pressure points. The pressure points are the last 5% of any given technique - an added extra, not the reason for the technique's existence.

Consequences

Pressure points can be a more humane way of suspending violence than hitting someone hard. Your attacker's broken nose is a fairly obvious sign that you hit your opponent, but a knockout at GB20 or closing down of S9 is less obvious. In these days of criminals breaking into people's homes, getting hit and then successfully suing the home-owner for GBH it is wise to have as much of the "necessary force" law on our side as possible.

Also, should it be made known that you are a martial artist, experienced or not, the powers-that-be automatically assume that you know what you are doing and what the result of your actions will be in matters of self-defence. That means that when you are woken up in the middle of the night by someone dressed in black snooping around your house, going through your things you are supposed to take their safety into account before you respond to the threat they pose. You can't know what that threat level is, but you can only react, according to Britsh Law, with "appropriate force". You can be as outraged as you like at how unjust that is, but that is what is happening.

The consequence must be seriously considered in advance of any given situation.

Attackers under the effects of adrenaline or drugs have been known to fight on with blood pouring from their nostrils, but a neurological shut-down stops them from injuring themselves even more by continuing the assault. As long as we are conscientious of our obligation as martial artists to only use force in the direst of circumstances then we minimise the risk of accusation that we have used excessive force. Let's face it: someone of rash temper prone to hitting people is unlikely to take the time to research the applications and pressure points used in Bassai Dai. This means that only those of us with a calm demeanour and academic leaning will even be interested enough to read this far into the book.

Meridians

The meridians are known by their relation to an *organ* or *bowel* within the body (e.g.; Liver, or Large Intestine), and the points along the meridian bear a number—how far they are from the end/beginning (Liver 6, Large Intestine 10 etc.).

The meridians are
Lung **LU**, Liver **LV**, Kidner **K,** Spleen **SP**, Heart **H**, Pericardium **PC,**
Large Intestine **LI**, Gallbladder **GB**, Bladder **BL**, Stomach **S**, Small Intestine **SI,**
Triple Warmer **TW**

Two major meridians which do not share this link to specific bowels and organs are the Conception vessel and the Governor vessel—two major energetic systems which are susceptible to disruption. (Although it could be argued that GV is the brain meridian and CV is the genital meridian.)

There are other meridians, known as the Extraordinary Vessels, but the complicated relationship is best explained elsewhere.

We will refer to points throughout the applications as places that can be struck, rubbed, or seized to make the application better. That doesn't mean that if you miss the point the application won't work, it merely means that when you do get the point you get a better result for less effort.

You also get a nice visualisation tool for the effect you are seeking to create:

The Oriental Medicine Theory of **Five Elements** suggests that the Ki which flows through the body possesses qualities similar to the elements **Fire**, **Water**, **Metal**, **Earth**, and **Wood**.

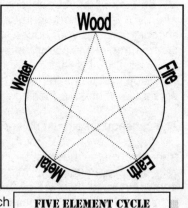

FIVE ELEMENT CYCLE

This gives us a clue as to how those elements interact and how the body may be affected by striking certain areas. To make matters even more complicated, each element will have at least one meridian each aligned with positive or negative energy, designated *Yin* or *Yang*. The exceptions are once again the Governor and Conception Vessels which comprise elements of all types and complete a Yin-Yang "circuit" which originates and ends at the same point for both

alignments making a written definition difficult.
The meridians can be classified as follows:

Lung **LU**, Yin Metal
Large Intestine **LI**, Yang Metal
Liver **LV**, Yin Wood
Gallbladder **GB**, Yang Wood
Kidner **K,** Yin Water
Bladder **BL**, Yang Water
Spleen **SP**, Yin Earth
Stomach **S**, Yang Earth
Heart **H**, & Pericardium **PC,** both Yin Fire
Small Intestine **SI, &** Triple Warmer **TW,** both Yang Fire

Each element has a pair, one yin, one yang of meridians (Fire has two pairs).

This is a broad topic, and the relationships of the elements and their points and meridians are beyond the scope of this manual, which practitioners are encouraged to seek out further information on. Suffice to say that the outer circle is the normal energetic cycle for Ki and is known as the **Natural Cycle of Enhancement**.

The normal flow may be thought of as Wood feeds Fire which feeds the Earth which makes Metal which may possess qualities of Water (think of mercury) which feeds Wood.

Hitting pressure points in the order they occur on the "Creative Cycle" might be thought of as building up the levels of damage consecutively. It activates pain in the order that would normally be gaining in strength. You might think of "pushing" Ki along the cycle faster or harder that it usually goes produces an overload in the body's energetic system (think of a Dam bursting). Similarly, blocking the natural flow of ki creates a weakness in the cycle and a "backwash" along the reverse of the route.

The way that the Elements are joined together within the Enhancement Cycle (in what looks like a star-shape) on the chart can be thought of as the **Cycle of Destruction**.

This may be thought of as Fire melts Metal which cuts Wood which pierces the Earth (think of a stake) which contains (dams) Water which extinguishes Fire.

The effect of one Element upon another when they are not meant to be joined in such a way can be likened to a "short circuit". Strangely enough the pain is usually described as "electrical". Note that the cycle of destruction is not simply a reversal of the natural cycle.

The elemental areas of our diagram are joined together by lines in our applications. These lines suggest the direction that the cycle is affected in, and which element affects which other element. Sometimes a broken line has been used to suggest alternatives where more than one application has been given or a supplementary part of the technique is illustrated.

At the end of the applications section there are a set of illustrations showing the location of the points mentioned in the text. These are to remind those who have already experienced the use of points as to the locations, and by no means show a complete topography of the meridians or their elemental/organic links. Remember, illustrations don't show contours like a human body properly.

One might suggest that the best technique includes an energetic strike to a susceptible set of pressure points, working along the five element cycle at opposite sides (yin-yang) of the body. Sometimes not all of these factors will be available, or the other factors which we regularly inject into our training (breath, heavy hand, BAR, etc) but the more we train them to exist in all of our techniques the more likely it will be that at least some of them will appear when we need them most.

If any of this seems bizarre then we would urge you to practise with us personally so that we can present the reasons for these things and demonstrate how they work.

The only way to really learn about any of this is with an instructor.

Principles

Throughout this work we make reference to certain principles and effects which are considered vital to **all** martial arts. These need to be explained properly to students, but are reviewed here to remind practitioners of the salient points.

As always, in text it is hard to describe something essentially physical. These things need to be shown and experienced for them to be understood. However, we'll do our best to remind practitioners of things which they should be constantly practising.

These factors can usually be applied to every technique, regardless of whether it is a strike, a throw, or a grapple. Principles remain principles no matter what situation is occurring; hence Funakoshi Gichin's maxims:

> *Transform yourself according to your opponent.*

And

> *Do the kata correctly, the real fight is a different matter.*

These principles should be relevant regardless of "style" or "association".

Once again we must emphasise that it is too much to expect someone to think of these things in the middle of a confrontation; we must train these factors in all of our regular classes until they become second nature and we do not have to think about them.

Line Theory

When we consider someone attacking us we usually find that they will allow themselves the most options to hit us as they possibly can. This means that they will aim all of their limbs (weapons) at us. This will manifest as the centre of their body aimed directly towards us.

When an opponent's centre is aimed towards us and our centre is aimed towards the opponent we are centre to centre—this is **"on-line"**. When the opponent has their centre aimed away from our centre (such as when we move out of their way) we consider ourselves to be **"off-line"**.

When two opponents are on-line the faster or stronger one will win. These are not good odds. The scientific martial artist seeks to have as many factors **in their favour** as possible.

A little bit of common sense tells us that when our centre is aimed at our opponent but their centre is not aimed at us that we can hit them but they are disadvantaged towards hitting us. We are on-line for striking them, they are off-line for striking us.

Ideally, we have all of our limbs (weapons) aimed at our opponent and they have none of theirs aimed at us. This gives us the most options and them the least. This way we are safer and can take more appropriate steps to deal with an opponent rather than the bone-crushing impact which might otherwise be our only recourse.

Whether someone has used a hook punch, straight punch, push, or grab; it is inadvisable to stand toe-to-toe and slug it out with them. It might not always be possible to get "off-line" with an opponent, but if we can we should.

We might consider "*the Martial Arts*" to be the skills associated with making as many things wrong for our opponent while keeping as many advantages for ourselves as possible. We might consider the "missing part" of every kata move to be "***Get Out of the Way***"; and this is clearly a demonstration of understanding line theory.

Stance Applications.

Stances may sometimes appear to be rigid ways of standing that Karate-ka use to distinguish themselves from other fighters. Nothing could be further from the truth.

Stances merely represent the application of body-weight into a technique: Back stance means keep your weight **back**. Front stance means push your weight **forwards**. Horse stance means drop your weight **down**.

The illusion comes from incorrect distance. Remember that a technique is committed *in the middle* of the whole movement, not at the end; so most of the time the end position or stance will never be reached.

Sometimes a grip and stance alone is all you need to have an effective technique. Throughout this work you will notice that stances are not often adhered to for applications. As mentioned above stance is the application of body-weight, so where it has not been necessary to use the weight it hasn't been used. This doesn't mean that the average or small practitioner shouldn't use their weight—it is an integral part of the technique and must not be overlooked. Big people must be *more careful* to not hurt their partner in practice by throwing their weight onto fragile joints and pressure points.

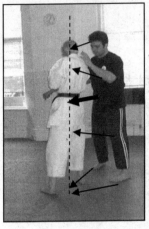

Point Everything at the Core.

When working on the attacker, both feet and both hands should be pointed at the core of the opponent in order for the technique to be most effective. It is easily provable that people are weaker with their feet aimed outwards. Pointing everything you have towards one point concentrates your power on that point.

If you cannot hit the opponent with either hand or either foot then you are reducing your options and therefore your chances of success. Maximise your options and your chances by directing everything towards your opponent's spine. In this way they can be struck with the shortest route and most direct line of impact (no need to twist your knees in order to strike).

Use Both Hands

Competition punches tend to withdraw quickly, or "bounce".

When we first examine a kata we must check our findings with some common sense. One of the questions we always ask is "What is the "*other*" hand doing?" It is usually fairly obvious that one hand will be contacting an opponent in one way or another, but the other hand must not be neglected. It must contain something or be attached to the opponent in some way. The use of a *hikite* (returning) hand greatly changes most applications that you can think of.

When first checking an application place one of the opponent's wrists in the hikite hand. There are times when it will be an elbow or head, but as soon as a wrist is placed there the application begins to materialise.

In obtaining that wrist there must first be some form of aggression toward you which you evade and parry then claim the attacking limb. Never losing contact with it (***muchimi***) is very different from just reaching out and magically grabbing the attacker's fist. It is an art unto itself.

Heavy Hand

We need to "penetrate"

Nearly every strike that is achieved in Karate, let alone this kata, needs to penetrate the target. This is achieved by hitting before the end of the technique (you can't penetrate if your arm is at maximum extension, nor if you bounce off the target). The weapon, the hand in this case, is allowed to drive deep into the attacker, making the strike a lot more than the superficial techniques used in competition.

This is adequately described as "heavy hand". Your strike should feel wet and heavy. We often tell students who appear too tense to wave their hand in the air and imagine that it weighs as much as the heaviest thing they can think of before striking—call it mental conditioning if you will. Once proficient at conjuring this imagery the "hand-waving" can be ignored in favour of just going straight into the activity.

The use of heavy hand does not rely upon strength; in many ways it is better to be "relaxed" <see *controlled pliability*>. Remember if Karate was only any good with strength then only the strong would be any good at Karate. This means that if you are small or not physically strong you cannot do Karate well - yet some of the most famous Karate Masters were known to have been sickly weak individuals who learned Karate so that they could not be taken advantage of. Work the technique, don't strong-arm it.

Controlled Pliability

Whereas the term *relax* may be taken to mean that you are sat at home with a packet of crisps in front of the TV, controlled pliability correctly gets across the idea that instead of tense muscular action we move fluidly without trying to match an opponent's physical strength.

Continuous movement with an integrated body means that small arm muscles are backed up by bigger, stronger leg muscles. Momentary yielding and re-direction will always be more tactically sound than matching muscle with muscle.

Give a Little to Get a Little

When meeting resistance we need to momentarily go with the direction of the resistance before working against it. We cannot rely upon strength.

We are unlikely to be attacked by someone who is obviously weaker than us; so when someone stronger than us tries to pull us in a particular direction or resist us pulling them in a particular direction then we simply give in (momentarily and only slightly) before continuing with our initial plan.

Resistance is "a use of muscle to prevent a course of action in a contra-direction"; to go with that direction momentarily will distract and disable the

Large circular movements are easily resisted or rely on muscular strength rather than technique

Small Circle Big Result

Tighter circles produce more dramatic results

Where a circle is called for (and what movement isn't circular in one way or another?) then the smaller the circle the bigger the result will be..

Any circular action that is large will telegraph the motion and allow the opponent to resist with muscular strength. Once again we are reminded that the attacker will probably be stronger than us, or "charged up" on adrenaline or other substances so that they feel stronger than us.

If it relies on strength it will not be possible to overcome someone of greater strength - technique must prevail, not power!

The more suddenly we begin a circle and the tighter we make it, the less resistance an opponent can apply. This should be a fluid circle which is not isolated to just a limb, but simultaneously uses the torque of the hips and a change in balance to accomplish a result.

Leave No Gap

Often the smallest gap can allow an attacker to wriggle or can prevent you from applying the correct amount of pressure. We see this time and time again; whenever a student cannot make a technique work this is often the first thing to correct.

It may sound strange to someone who wishes to avoid being hit, but truthfully; the further away you keep an opponent's limb the harder it will be to manipulate it.

Should you take hold of the opponent but allow an air pocket between your palm and their wrist you will need more strength to make a technique work. Should you wish to throw someone over your hip then your hip needs to be in contact (no gap). Yet people will end up struggling because they haven't got in close enough to do the throw easily.

Angle & Direction

Every technique is applied at particular angles to the opponent's body. Every technique is applied in a particular direction. Although this principle applies to every technique in this manual it is a huge subject which can only be adequately taught and **corrected** in a lesson/dojo environment.

The direction that a limb/body is struck in can have a huge effect. There are directions that the body can take punishment in and directions that the body is weaker in; obviously it is important that you train to impact the areas in the correct manner so that you don't have to rationalise it during a confrontation.

As a general rule, to enhance any technique apply it at *45 degrees* to the opponent and work *through* them.

Mind Breath Body

This is probably the most important principle of all.

Every move must be performed with intention (mind). That doesn't mean that you must carefully think of each movement before you do it, that would be too slow. It means that you must intend to perform the strike or manoeuvre to the very best of your ability.

As you make any manoeuvre you expel the air in your body through your mouth (breath). This produces a tension in the *hara* and prevents you from being winded should you be struck at the same time. (You can't tense your nose, you might as well tense your tum.) The tension is momentary not prolonged, and it occurs only at the **end** of your technique. Any prolonged tension will slow you down. At the time of the breath being exhaled there should be a momentary touch of the tongue to the roof of the mouth (just behind the teeth). This is accomplished by soundlessly shaping the word *hut* as you breath. This completes an energetic cycle within the body, linking the Conception Vessel and the Governor Vessel and increases the body's power without any extra effort.

Having intention and having breathed before the end of the move the **body** is finally committed to the move. You intend the move as you begin it, you breath and then you commit the act. Mind breath body—in that order.

Of course, the whole sequence happens very quickly, but if you concentrate on this in every lesson you do it becomes a trained sequence and finally a subconscious sequence. You will find that even the simplest exercises become trials of concentration while this factor is being drilled.

The OODA Loop

If we are to base our work on the assumption that the movements in the kata are indeed for use in potentially dangerous situations, then it is worth studying the way that the brain organises events.

Writers like Geoff Thompson have labelled much of what happens to the body quite thoroughly. The OODA loop was the label that Colonel John R. Boyd gave to the decision making process in military strategy. He believed it was applicable in all situations.

OODA is **Observe—Orient—Decide—Act**.

Observation could be classed as awareness rather than the act of sight, followed by the positioning of the body and the mind labelled here as orientation. The decision to act must be a quick one, programmed into the body through training, and then the action must be a decisive and applicable one.

Observation is the act of rising through the colour-coded levels that Geoff Thompson codifies for us, changing from *relaxed* to *potential* mode and then, if the movements are needed, to an *actual* mode of engagement.

Orientation is taking into account what the body's chemistry is going through in order to assess and be *able* to appropriately respond.

Decision is the over-coming of the fight/flight/freeze internal battle that we all go through when confronted by aggression. Hopefully our introspective tendencies and training amount to the right decision in the right circumstance.

The **Action** must, of course, be appropriate to the level of threat presented.

The reason that the process is a loop is that the *actions* will inform a whole new *observation* and *awareness* of unfolding events; just as a decision may change circumstances and any outside information/data gathered as the system progresses can cause a re-assessment of the situation. The development of the situation may lead to a more dire need on the part of the defender, or it might lead to a de-escalation of aggression.

Now, the problem for the martial artist is that this whole sequence, that a military strategist could have sat down and had meetings about, must occur in a fraction of a second. The aggressor isn't going to give you time to ponder your tactics.

It might be considered that all of this merely complicates matters and actually hinders the decision making process. The only thing that stands in it's favour is the idea that, like the samurai of old, one must think through one's actions and their consequences well in advance, and the OODA loop might be just the qualitative and quantitative reckoner that we require.

Russell Stutely has a phrase "You will do most often what you most often do".

In any self-defence situation the way your body will react is the way it has been trained to react. If you are left with non-reaction (which might be appropriate in the case of only verbal aggression) you will be in a spot of bother with physical aggression. It has been seen many times; the unaware innocent who is picked on by a Neanderthal can do nothing while the other lays into them. If they had only trained their brain to assess the situation sooner, and had a little physical training to at least "not get hit", then they might survive better.

SENSIBLE POINTS

The movements that we make in kata are symbolic short-hand of complete methods of fighting. We know this to be true or each kata would include running away, arguments, distractions and mis-directions, and buying the other party a drink just to stop any escalation of the situation. Those who mis-understand kata, or who have only an understanding of the shapes without their meanings, often miss the things which kata DO NOT show.

Combative applications require COMMON SENSE put in front of them. This means that if an application goes against the laws of physics or human biology (whether described by oriental or occidental medicine) then it is WRONG.

Kata applications must work against anyone of any size, using common anatomical weaknesses as the targets of common anatomical weapons. This means that a small woman must be able to successfully use the applications against bigger men.

In truth, the application to any move in a kata can be anything that you want it to be. The key is that YOU must be able to use it that way. There is no point in some senior grade insisting that a move can only be used in a particular way if that way is beyond your capabilitites.

In many ways the first recourse is to strike. The moral implications for this are for the individual to work through in their own mind. Sometimes striking may not be practical, or the "usual" occidental fist-based strike may not be viewed favourably (such as when cctv is involved or when observed by others).

Many of the karate movements have a non-aggressive appearance: to the world at large even a neck-wrench does not *appear* as violent as a repetitive fist impacting on a face.

Many of the techniques can be applied with varied levels of force, so if only a little force is required then that is all that you need to use, but if increased force is required then that is what you *may* choose to use.

Over the page you will find what we consider to be Sensible Points. When people turn up for training they usually just want to learn punches and kicks, but it is important that everyone understands that rehearsing these points is also an important part of training.

The ground rules:

- **If you can avoid the confrontation, do.**

- **If you can talk your way out of it before it gets messy, do.**

- **If you can hit then escape, pre-emptively or otherwise, do.**

- **If you hit an attacker and it doesn't finish it then use the time you buy yourself to use your technique. An aggressor will be more compliant if you have already hit him.**

- **If one technique does not fulfill your requirements use another. Don't stop. Carry on until you are safe. Kata applications show a snap shot of action, not the whole fight.**

- **If you can, move to a position of relative safety/strength (off-line rather than directly in front of his "other" fist).**

- **Safety first. Practice the moves with speed, power, and visualisation only on a bag or thin air, not on a partner. This is what kata are for. When practicing on empty air don't lock out joints, use your muscles to stop the movement.**

The Usual Suspects

In the following section we present a series of applications for the moves in the kata. These applications are a mixture of what "other teachers" might teach and what we do.

The other teachers' works have all been presented in other Karate and Kata books or been taught at seminars by high ranking karateka (5th, 6th, 7th, and 8th Dans) including some Japanese. By no means did these people suggest that these were the _only_ explanations available (to their credit) but neither did they suggest that these were merely exercises to improve timing, strengthen limbs, etc. These are honest representations of the *bunkai* of other teachers.

Our aim is to show that these applications are not **sensible**.

We do not seek to embarrass or upset, but merely present the reasons why this type of bunkai should not be taught. If we cause one practitioner to actively question their art and research deeper then we will have succeeded.

Even if a practitioner does not like our alternatives to the applications, at least they will begin to delve into what the applications might be **for them**. You see, the further into practising the martial arts we get, the more we come to realise that this is an entirely personal journey. You don't practice to make someone else proud of you (though it's nice if that happens); you don't practice to be better than someone else (inevitably, they are always better at *something* than you are); you only practice as long as you are happy to do so. If you seek self defence and all you are doing is sport you will leave. If you want sport and all you do is basics you will (eventually) leave. If you are being taught something which in your heart you recognise as nonsense then you will not listen for long.

Those that leave because they feel "something is missing" are a loss to the world of martial arts. They walk away telling people that "Karate doesn't work" when the truth is that they just haven't seen Karate appropriate to their demands.

Inevitably there will be criticism from some quarters as to our need to show these things as unworkable. Some will say "live-and-let-live", and that if a school wishes to use applications which don't work then it is none of our business. This is fine as long as the instructor doesn't present the information as though it is usable self-defence.

Many schools operate as a "cult of personality" where something *must* be true because the big-shot top-dog says it is. Unfortunately, the students of that teacher will probably never get to see anything other than that man's teachings.

There will be a school of thought which states that when we are as competent in the martial arts as the teachers who show these applications then we won't need to scorn these applications. When we are good enough, we will be able to see the genius of these people's work and we will be able to **make** it work. If we are not shown workable and competent applications to begin with then how are we ever to become competent at anything more than making good shapes in the air?

The idea that one must train for years before something will work is unfeasible.

Why not show techniques which will work from the beginning, but the more experience you have the easier /better it becomes?

Why not add the complicated moves later, when one is more able of mind and body and ready to delve deeper into our studies?

There will be another school of thought which maintains that *their* school doesn't do such stupid applications and that even our *favoured* applications which follow the next section are inferior to theirs. To this group we say "GREAT!". You obviously have a good teacher and belong to a group who are honest and interested in their art. Please don't think that our alternative applications are the only ones we practice—we teach at least three workable variations for every technique in every kata—it's just that these are reasonable and can be presented in print without too much in the way of explanation.

So, if the applications we present as the work of others seem ridiculous to you and you've never been taught anything so stupid then count yourself lucky. There really are a huge number of schools out there for whom this is karate!

These applications share some common themes—the attacker starts from an unreasonable distance away; the attacks are martial artists' trained attacks (not the common type of attack which occurs); stances are often irrelevant to what occurs with the body and arms; and the attacker is rarely effectively prevented from continuing with his assault.

EXPLODING MYTHS

One of the biggest fallacies about the ready position of this kata is that it represents a greeting or courtesy - it is a technique! No-one has ever seen Japanese people greet each other with the first movement of Bassai Dai.

If the kata's originators don't do it then why should *we* (the inheritors of the tradition) think it is a salutation?

If kata represent the culmination and encryption of a past master's knowledge why would they begin the kata with anything other than a common form of self -defence?

One might argue that they would begin with a posture for mental preparation, solemnity, and correcting of any character flaws one might possess. We must remember that the character development and introspective side of our art is a by-product of austere conditioning, and a fairly modern reason for training.

Although martial artists have generally been of historically good character, such was by no means the *reason* for training. Teachers such as **Itosu Ankho** may have required that his students be of good character, but the idea that training would make one into a good person only really arrived when Itosu campaigned for Karate to be included within the Okinawan school curriculum. This was posited as being necessary for the building of courageous citizens of Okinawa so that they would be strong enough in body and mind to make good soldiers. The logic in this argument really goes against the foundation of "*martial artists will have good character*" and instead promotes nationalism!

Understand that at the time of this promotion of Karate-do there was a need for Okinawan citizens to be seen to embrace the Japanese culture and standards so that they might be accepted (or *not persecuted*) by the Japanese.

The common form of courtesy being a bow, in modern Japan it may just be a slight nod of the head. For budoka, the bow is normally performed from the hips. Opinions differ about eye-contact/head position. Staring at someone may be confrontational; dipping the head may result in an unexpected attack. Keeping the eyes aimed at the opponent's chest may seem wise until one is partnered with a female; so keeping **zanshin** and staring all-round and past the opponent may be more practical.

The bow is all that one needs in order to affect mental preparedness. The fixing of the breath and mindset are not accomplished through clasping of your own hand in front of you.

If the clasped fist were to be regarded as "just a ready position" then why not begin all kata with the same ready position?

Why is Bassai Dai different to all other kata in the Shotokan system?

Some have suggested that the opening shape is symbolic of "*Karate* (the fist) *is my secret* (hidden in the other hand)".

This seems very poetic, but becomes so secret that those teachers have forgotten another maxim of Karate: there are no wasted movements! The only place you could make such a statement would be in the dojo, surrounded by other practitioners, who hopefully the art is not a secret from anyway.

Others have suggested that this is a link back to the Shaolin Temple origins of the kata. Shaolin monks will only use this kind of posture if they are martial artists, and it must be remembered that the only Shaolin monks you will see are those practising WuShu—the government sponsored Martial Art of China. There is no suggestion that WuShu is not valid, or worthy, or that those monks are tough and acrobatic; just that this cannot be said to be the "original martial arts" that we are supposed to look for a link to. There is no evidence that Bhodidharma (Daruma) ever taught martial arts to the monks, nor that those same skills transferred to Okinawa and became Karate.

Certainly Okinawans learned from Chinese, just as they learned from Japanese, but they would also have known how to fight before such cross-pollination. Certainly the exchange of information would have taken place and no doubt helped to shape Karate, but it cannot be said to be Kung Fu/ Chuan Fa taught the Okinawan way.

The next fallacy is that the next sequence takes us towards an attacker who threatens us from 6 feet away. Obviously he can punch as hard as he likes and not hurt us at this distance, so why would we block? And would we block with our hands in this configuration? To block here means that you have to go towards the danger to stop it—hardly wise.

It has been reported that the "assisting hand" makes the block stronger! This type of pressing motion is only of use in assisting a slower arm movement than is presented in the kata and would not be used against the punch which is usually presented (as here). Assisting this way looks like some kind of "cheat" for arm-wrestling.

All the talk of charging in and seizing the initiative does not make sense if all you are going to seize it with is a block? Wouldn't you seize the initiative by striking?

Let's have a look at some answers.

Consider an opponent who waves their fist and is preparing to strike you. This kind of situation occurs in the "interview" stage of a confrontation. For further reading on the anatomy of a confrontation there is no better analysis than that of **Geoff Thompson**. Everyone interested in self protection should read his books.

1) The aggressor is threatening you , waving their left hand in your face as they posture and ready themselves with their right (The opponent is *most* likely to use their left hand to gesture as they are most likely to want to **hit** with their right).

If you are to end the situation quickly with a pre-emptive strike, you would have to believe that you were in imminent danger in order to justify using karate on them.

Seize the wrist with your right hand and then the back of their hand with your left.

Capturing a wrist is easiest when approached through the "shadow of the hand". In the situation illustrated the right hand approaches the wrist through an *unseen* route - the opponent's own arm blocks his vision.

If the left hand tried to grab the wrist the opponent would simply take his hand away and hostilities would commence sooner rather than later.

Once the latch has been obtained then we are already moving into the realms of controlling the opponent; we have certainly changed their game plan from their expected outcome (they expected to just

hit you!). Placing the other hand on the opponent should occur immediately after the latch is achieved.

If at all possible, cover the wrist pressure points (Lung 9, Heart 7, Small Intestine 5, and Large Intestine 5) and create a leverage-bridge; simultaneously cover Large Intestine 3 with the other hand.

The only time you would use *two* arms against one is when you are sure that the movement will prevent them from striking with their other hand.

Pull down, with a slight twist towards the hara. This causes the opponent's arm to cross his centre-line and so turns his body. This position closely resembles the starting position of Bassai Dai. As you can see, sometimes it is all that is needed.

Cross-body motor reaction is what causes the opponent's other arm to go away. This is important as it was their intention to hit you with that hand.

Consider the "whiplash" on the neck from a sudden motion. The shoulder's rotator cuff may also be damaged. The attacker is in a vulnerable position.

Please note that there is no attempt to rely on strength to accomplish this technique, it is achieved by practiced accuracy and the use of body mechanics.

The verbal distraction, timing, and any other distraction methods which you deem appropriate can be used to again the advantage. Remember that a partner in training who can lock their arm so that you cannot do this to them has not attacked you, and is not trying to bypass your grab, they are busy immobilising it.

Principles such as

Give a little to get a little
Small circle, big result
Mind breath body

are much more important than being physically gifted; after all you are unlikely to be attacked by someone who does not think they have a chance of hurting you.

When we analyse whether or not this could be *bunkai* or *oyo* of the first move of Bassai Dai we may take a few pointers into consideration:

- The kata tells us that a fist is covered over the back of the hand.
- The originators encoded a feet-together position to illustrate (perhaps) that no "weight application" was necessary for this move.
- There is no oriental salutation that matches this position.
- This application does not rely upon a "Karate attack" or the opponent beginning 2 metres away.
- At the end of the application the opponent is in no condition to carry on without encountering immediate further resistance. They are in a seriously disadvantaged position.

continued

In this example we have continued the motion to include a pull back towards the hip—further disrupting the opponent's balance—and a raised knee to the vulnerable rib area (gallbladder/liver crossing if possible) followed by a push over.

If you failed to contact the ribs you would be certain to contact the outer thigh (dead leg point GB31). This could be accompanied by a "gooseneck" lock if one were so predisposed. Although difficult to achieve, trapping the opponent's leg whilst "storming forwards" would enable an easier push.

In Oriental medicine, this conforms to the destructive cycle FIRE MELTS METAL CUTS WOOD. The fire and metal points are located on the attacker's wrist, the wood points are on the ribs. The order that the points are struck in reveals extra weakness in the latter points.

The corkscrew motion of the wrist utilises quadrant theory and the motion is one of yielding followed by overcoming—Yin & Yang.

Observe how neither person begins in a "Yoi" position, nor at such a range as to make the strike and the defence impractical. Without a defence the attacker would very easily cause damage in the above scenario (unlike many bunkai which seem to use kumite distance only). Also see how the attacker's other limb goes away whilst the manipulation occurs. This is a natural event which helps to demonstrate the effectiveness of the technique.

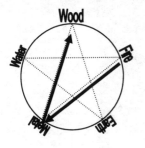

Sequence 1

ALTERNATIVE

This supplementary version shows how an attacker tries to prevent someone from leaving an altercation. Consider that all attempts at talking the situation down have failed and you have tried to turn to leave but the aggressor isn't going to let you. They have reached out to grab the defender to pull him back into the situation and into their control.

The simple turn of their wrist and suppression of their grasp runs through the same factors as listed above. This bunkai works with cross-arm or two handed grabs.

Anyone who has attended one of the OCI seminars will recognise the application of "centre-lock" through this version of the kata. Aikido people might call the technique a variation of *nikkyo*, but to me it will always be Basai uke.

The more complex the lock (- the more angles created in the attacker's arm -) the more pain will be inflicted.

continued

Caution: like all the techniques shown here, this one is simple and destructive. Take great care of your partner's wrist when training. It is a small matter of degrees between pain and break, always err on the side of caution.

The feeling of pushing forward can be experimented with to incorporate

• the dropping of one's weight,

• a tight spiral motion that totally overwhelms the attacker,

• secondary impacting of the knee into the opponent's inner thigh or knee,

• or simply the trapping of the opponent's foot (try stepping on it)

The technique is not accomplished with brute strength, but rather by twisting the body and arm at the same time. The opponent may seek to control your movement when they grab your wrist, but that does not stop your hips from moving.

The aggressor, as shown here, has a natural instinct to raise their elbow to protect their joints. In training this might be allowed to prevent harm, but if the situation warranted it then the elbow can be bought down, either by making the turn of the body tighter, or by crashing our own elbow down on top of it. This is likely to separate the bones of the wrist, so once again, training partners should be warned against exuberance.

This is a basic application for the kosa-dachi stance. Where ever you find it think of twisting on the spot or as you move in that direction.

On top of everything else, the sheer shock of seeing you attempt to leave and then having you come straight back in will seriously disturb the aggressor's plans. It wasn't what they had in mind.

To talk of the next sequence as consisting of "double blocks" means that the masters have supplied us with kata which do not show how to retaliate.

Would you block two attacks then turn and block another two attacks without effectively dealing with the first attacker?

This also does not deal with the idea of how one becomes *aware* enough to know when someone is about to punch us.

Just by looking at the pictures here you can see that for the blocks to contact in their usual way the distance actually means that no *turn* is necessary as no *block* is necessary! He can't hit you from that distance, and at the distance he *can* hit you from behind *you can't block* in that fashion.

2) An incoming arm (fist/push/grab etc) may be intercepted in so many different ways.

Bassai Dai provides a sequence of three variations for the same thing: the "turning blocks" sequence. In a predominantly linear style of karate this set of moves illustrates multiple uses of small circles.

Our first example uses the case of an attacker from the rear grasping the shoulder.

Thinking the situation through, what we are observing is what happens after the initial verbage. The defender is again trying to leave a situation. Perhaps he has inadvertently offended the attacker who now wishes to rearrange his features; the ego of the attacker means that they turn the "victim" so that they are a) surprised, b) witness to who this master of intimidation is.

The attacker intends to turn the victim and strike him.

Looking over the shoulder does not give a lot of time to assess the situation, and a small sliding motion away from the danger opens up the distance (*maai*) to earn an extra second of response time.

Locating/fixing the hand on the shoulder is vital as it
a) provides a "base" for the rest of the technique,
b) prevents that hand from being used to strike you.

Uchiuke=arm bar from inside
Hikite = retaining hand

A simple arm bar striking TW11 looks much the same as Uchi-uke (Note how the technique uses 2 arms: one from under the other). The alleged "withdrawing" hand is used to locate, set, and pull on the attacker's grabbing hand.

At the very least you have already changed their "game-plan" from being an instant mugging to being a situation that they will have to re-assess.

The second (gyaku) Uchi-uke is used as a strike.

Targets for the strike will depend large-ly upon how big the opponent is and how badly they are affected by the arm-bar. The target used here is Lu1, used to off-balance the opponent and cause pain until they can either be restrained or struck again. Other targets may include the supra-sternal notch (CV22) or the jawline (S4,5, or 6), or virtually anywhere on the neck (normally striking S9 and/or LI18).

The clue here is that performing the move in the kata will work. The targets that present themselves are those that the opponent shows/gives you —and this will vary with the size and responsiveness of the opponent. In training we have seen everything from impact on the pec-toral muscle (not the best place), to hitting the nose and even the temple with this same shot. How you use your hips will have a lot to do with it.

Here we find that we have a FIRE & METAL + FIRE + METAL combination.

Again, it is worth noting that cross-body motor reaction causes the potential strike to actually move *away* from it's target.

Gyaku-uchiuke = strike
Hikite = retaining hand

This early on in the kata we also run into the issue of **line**. The way that these attacks are presented usually shows blocks working against straight attacks of the kind which only another martial artist would perform. The "arm-pounding" which goes on here may be argued for as a way of conditioning the body to bear heavy impacts; however these type of attacks do not fall into the category of those we might ***reasonably expect to encounter***.

When we consider that the techniques of Bassai Dai would not win us any Kumite (sparring) tournaments then we know that they cannot be used against other martial artists. This leaves us with using them against non-martial artists. Assuming that we are not training to go out and pick fights with innocents, we must be using our Karate against those who would attack us.

This all seems quite obvious, but then we must take the leap of faith acknowledging that the attacks the kata was formulated to prevent or retaliate to will not be Karate attacks - they will be the common type of punches, grabs, and kicks which non-trained people will commit.

Just to really spell it out: - if the bunkai shown use Karate attacks then the bunkai is flawed.

Patrick McCarthy Kyoshi uses a wonderful term: the *Habitual Acts of Physical Violence*. He has deduced from his years of research that there are 36 HAPV with 72 variations. For bunkai to have been thought out properly it must respond to one of the HAPV or be pre-emptive!

In any type of non pre-arranged combat we are better off avoiding the direct line of attack by removing our body from it and simultaneously warding or parrying. This significantly reduces the chance of being struck by removing targets from the attacker's range. Meeting attacks head-on means that the faster and/or stronger fighter will win. No-one can *reasonably* expect to be attacked by someone who is weaker and/or slower than themselves. If you should be attacked by someone weaker, slower, and smaller than yourself you have no business using Karate on them.

Bio-mechanically it is not the most sensible thing to receive impact on only one bone of the arm, either. *Soto uke* takes the impact on the small bone of the fore-arm (ulna) and *uchi uke* receives the impact on the large bone (radius) should straight attacks be met head on as shown here. With just a little *taisabaki* (taking us *off-line*) we find that at the crucial moment both types of block use both bones to make their connection with the attacker.

When the kata is considered as a database of techniques, would it not be reason-able to place a retaliation after this many blocks? If the kata is not a database but representative of a fight against many opponents then wouldn't the first attacker (who has not been dispatched) make a mess of the back of your head while the second attacker is being blocked?

It is for these reasons that many people cast aside kata—they have unreasonable expectations of what the kata represents. They grow disaffected with what the kata is popularly taught for (combat against multiple opponents) but does not ac-complish (it is unrealistic on that basis). Just look again at what the kata **can** do. It's much more impressive than some "Hollywood" style fight against 15 ninja.

Sotouke = outside arm-bar

A straight punch is deflected and pulled to the hip.

This uses a classical brush & latch movement which many people mistake to mean that we are able to catch a punch. This would be super human. Rather, we deflect the punch and maintain contact with it whilst we drag the hand down the arm until it comes to a natural stop at the wrist.

Traditional martial arts concepts of *kake* (hooking), and *muchimi* (sticking) are vital in training.

The thumb may or may not be engaged—it doesn't matter. You should certainly not *attempt* to grab using the thumb. Remember, engage the thumb means engage the brain, and this kind of situation does not allow you to engage the brain — it must be instinctive or trained.

The very act of pulling the opponent in may jar their neck. The whiplash that a strong *hikite* (pull) can cause can often be highly alarming to someone who didn't know it was coming.

The closer the opponent's arm is to your body the more of a reaction you cause by levering their arm against your (momentarily) tensed stomach (kime).

This also corresponds with the oft-

repeated advice that all karate movements use the hips for power. They certainly do if you rotate your body slightly into this attacker's elbow. No arm strength is required.

The defender brings their left arm up to bar the attacker's right arm and cut backwards into Triple Warmer 11/the golgi receptors of the elbow. This move looks just like Soto-uke.

It is the cutting action that activates the golgi receptors, effectively telling the brain that the arm has been broken. The subsequent release of tension and strength makes the opponent much more malleable.

We now have a good reason to twist the arm when executing this move - if it were just for stopping a punch we would be better off with the two bones of the forearm against the opponents arm.

The Uchi-uke is used to strike. The **whole** of the forearm is used to impact the attackers neck. When people ask about how you can hit something as small as a pressure point we use techniques like this one and shuto uke to ask how you can *miss* pressure points when your technique is at the correct distance and following on from a realistic attack.

Again, the target will depend upon how badly they are affected by the arm-bar. In this case the neck was reachable, striking S9 and LI18 with one shot. Even without this target becoming available a second bar against TW11 would be possible.

Uchiuke = strike
Hikite = retaining hand

continued

The forearm twisting into the movement is a technique enhancer. If we have struck the neck then this is an abrasive movement that feels like it "cuts" into the neck. If we have contacted the arm then this is the key to activating TW11 powerfully.

Note that in the example shown the stances given by the kata are not achieved. Stances are the final force multiplier—in practice we need to be able to achieve results without force for the sake of our training partner!

Force is easy to add in to a technique, and is achieved naturally as soon as you are under stress anyway. The results shown are achieved without the massive force prescribed by the use of stance.

The change of hand to capture the arm is a natural movement. Maintaining contact with the attacker's offered arm we simply swap hands to keep control of him. The one-two action (rather than repeatedly striking with one hand) allows the hip to be put into the second strike, keeping the power-level high. Striking again with the left hand would have required a pull-back motion, and hence, would have wasted a precious second.

This combination utilises a FIRE + METAL - EARTH elemental wave. The Fire points are TW11, the Metal points are LI18, and potential Earth points include S9

The next sequence is often referred to as catching a leg and then breaking the knee.

Firstly, it would be rare for someone to attack with anything that remotely resembled a front kick as we understand it. The front kick practiced in sport Karate is above the belt for the safety of the practitioners. You lose a touch of your balance and a proportion of power every time you raise your knee above belt height. It is good exercise to kick above the belt, but much more damaging below the belt. It also takes a long time to kick above the belt, whereas someone who is attacking you will want to kick you sharply and as a surprise.

Secondly, anyone who has ever tried the "usual application" will tell you that this is not the way to break someone's knee! And why would you need to block again following an opponent's knee being broken? The attacker must be virtually super-human to continue attacking with a broken knee. (Wouldn't it be easier to just move backwards, anyway?)

The timing represented here is not indicative of an attack from someone intent on doing you harm. The only way this application works is with someone of the same dojo who has been trained to attack so that they can be blocked (as opposed to attacking with the intention of doing harm).

Again we see that the distance from the first position to "safely" catch the kick means that you don't actually have to catch it at all - it doesn't reach you. The other flaw is the assumption of a set sequence of attacks - this bunkai doesn't work if the attacker decides to do two kicks instead of one, or if his second attack is a left hook, or...

When someone is really intent on kicking you we need to shift out of the way rather than relying on our arms to stop powerful legs from connecting with us. Just about everybody has bigger leg muscles than arm muscles. Leg muscles carry more weight and are stronger. We should not try to match the strength of our arms with the strength of someone else's legs, but evade.

People don't punch you in the feet and they don't kick you in the head if you are stood upright. (On the floor is another matter entirely.)

Altogether, this application ends up creating another false impression in the mind of the student.

In this scenario (being grabbed with both hands) it is necessary to avoid a potential head-butt or knee.

Many people think that your first priority should be the hands placed on you; yet these are not causing you harm, merely preventing the attacker from punching you.

The defender's right thumb knuckle is used to impact directly into the Liver/Gallbladder meridian crossing point. The Liver /Gallbladder crossing is important—it is a place where two meridians cross, both are of the Wood element, but one is Yang and one is Yin, one runs to the head, the other to the feet. This is a nice "short-circuit" place to hit.

The movement in the kata dictates the course and direction of the impact; using your fist as though it were an ice cream scoop to "cut" through the opponent's body.

This also causes the opponent to buckle slightly, altering his head and knee direction to off-line.

continued

Sukui uke = thumb-knuckle strike
Hikite = retaining hand

The stationary left hand throughout the first two parts of the technique is a give-away that you should pin the attacker's limb to you. This simple action of keeping the attacker's hand in place means that they are levered more easily. Pinning does not mean grabbing. Just placing your fist on top of their hand and squeezing it to you will keep it in place better than fiddling about with fingers and thumbs.

Some practitioners dip down very low just before the initial movement, allegedly catching a kick—another target which is available is GB31 (the Dead Leg point) and this dip signifies a drop to hit that point.

GB31 is a great target within the application as again it is a wood point, and as it is further from our next target we are using an enhanced quadrant theory for greater effect!

The lowering of your own head may not be the wisest thing to do, but you may find that with a pinned opponent or a loss of balance that this target naturally becomes available.

In practice, we seek to control the head by having it collide with our shoulder, but obviously the height of the attacker and speed of the technique will influence this.

continued

It is followed up directly with a hammer-fist attack to the jaw or neck.

If at all possible, we like to see this land at GB20, on the back of the head. This demonstrates our Quadrant Theory nicely, whether you have hit the GB/Liv crossing or GB31. By placing the forearm against the neck you usually find that your hammer-fist will be in place at the back of the skull.

The left arm can follow up with another strike to the neck, or bar against Triple Warmer 11 of a grabbing left hand.

As a combination, this set makes the defender swamp the attacker in a flurry of blows; a good tactic taking into account that some may miss etc. Another principle to follow is "*Don't stop until the job is done.*"

The elemental equation is the classical Fire melts Metal. Metal cuts Wood.

The Fire points are TW11 and the wrist points.
The Metal points are the wrist points.
The Wood points are the Liver/Gallbladder crossing and Gallbladder 31.

Sotouke = strike from outside
Uchiuke = strike from inside
Hikite = retaining hand

Sequence 5

The tate shutouke which seems to precede a punch which is then followed by a block makes a mockery of the idea that kata would decisively end a conflict.

Firstly, the distance is clearly incorrect for the attacker to attack. This punch did not have to be blocked. Then you have to ask whether you are likely to block a punch in this fashion at all. You are not. It isn't a natural reflex and it isn't even a trained version of a reflex.

The stepping/lunge punch is not the type of attack that you are likely to encounter outside the dojo. You could argue that this is merely a training method and that a shorter range punch is the follow-up after training. We would argue that you should begin with the technique that you expect to meet—if confidence is the issue then start slowly and build up speed, don't train one distance and expect an automatic transition to another.

The first block is followed by a punch, but the attacker is now magically closer to you, and the defender doesn't attempt to use his bodyweight in his retaliation at all, relying instead on the might of his arm. This is foolish to say the least.

If you hit someone then why do you need to subsequently block their next attack? Did you fail to hit them properly? This is, of course possible, but not something that the masters of old would codify for us to remember as a core article of their teaching.

Yes, if you fail to end the confrontation with one defence/retaliation then you must be prepared to continue; but this isn't a good reason for moves like this in kata.

Students should practice for success, not failure.

And when you block the second attack what is the hand on the hip doing?

Speaking of hips, this combination ignores the starting position of the hands placed at the hip. This ready position is apparently redundant. Why keep it then? (Answers over the page.)

If the attacker is able to attack again (necessitating your subsequent block) then why doesn't he just hit you again? If your blows are this ineffective why aren't you presented with an alternative strike which might do better (and not lead to you having to block further attacks)?

This type of programming does nothing for the student, leading to claims of "when you are a higher grade you will understand" and other such nonsense.

3) Though often overlooked, the starting "cup and saucer" position is actually an effective defence all on it's own!

Having avoided a punch by moving slightly sideways and forwards while deflecting, the attacking arm is latched and pulled to the hip. When moving in and forwards like this the parrying hand is across the body to cover as much target area as possible. It also leaves the right hand ready to strike, if that is the preferred option, in a direct manner.

The defender moves around so that their body produces leverage against the attacker's arm, otherwise it is all in the defender's arm-strength. Once located securely at the hip, the wrist is seized by the right hand and the fist bent upwards to gain compliance.

Usually, it will be found that the fist opens due to the energy flooding to the hand. Control of the wrist is achieved through the attacker feeling like he has "given up".

The short-circuit of the attacker's intention and subsequent concern for not having his face fall into the floor tend to manifest as a degree of compliance.

This is codified in the kata as a wrist at the hip with a hand placed at right-angles to it directly above it.

continued

Koshi gamae = wrist lock

This is a smooth continuous action that yields with an opponent's force and re-directs it to a position of relative security. The "*muchimi*" - sticking– sensation is better than grabbing. You train to stay in contact with the arm coming in rather than using your fingers and thumbs to engage them.

The location of the left elbow above the opponent's right elbow effectively prevents them from struggling.

If possible, we seek to put pressure on the LI3 point of the index knuckle.

Extra pressure can be applied, depending on the ability level of the defender by seizing the ring finger and little finger separately from the other two fingers and applying pressure on them at separate angles to the hand.

An important point to remember is to vary the pressure/pain applied to the joints, as any constant pain can eventually be resisted.

Note that the action of the kata takes place after having avoided an attack. And that the "turning-pulling up" motion is what achieves the result.

The defender's body is positioned so that it faces directly into the arm of the attacker. Where the attacker starts and finishes has no relevance to the facing of the move as performed in the kata.

The meridians affected are the fire meridians on the outside of the arm, and then, on the latching action we combine them with metal points to make our classic "Fire melts metal" combination.

Following on:

The "palming off" motion can be used to gain access to the very delicate area behind the jaw. If this movement is used as a strike then it is very effective. If this movement is used to manipulate the head then the hair or an ear can be grabbed to make it easier.

The palm itself, or the corner of the hand, (tate-shuto uke) is used with great effect either to the cluster of Gallbladder points above the temple; or if needed, against S4 to definitively turn the head.

The movement is away form your body, and moving through multiple angles—up, away, and twisting. If you just push you have more of a battle.

Turning an opponent's face away from you is one of the most fundamental things you can do in self-protection. It becomes very difficult for an opponent to bring pressure to bear if they cannot face you. It also makes breathing more laboured and blood-pressure rise as the neck is invariable constricted (even if only slightly). Most importantly, it stops Them from being in Control.

Once again we find that the kata provides us with direct angle and direction for an effective strike. This time it is to Triple Warmer 17 with the straight punch which follows.

continued

Tate shuto uke = head arrangement/strike
Chokuzuki = strike to jaw
Hikite = retaining hand

The "pulling back" motion (touch your thumb to your own chest) is a lateral vascular neck restraint (strangle/choke) which is quickly followed by another impact to TW17 on the other side of the opponent's head (which looks a lot like an "inside block" when the drill is performed without a partner).

The restraint can be used in a reasonably humane way by allowing the crook of the elbow to sit in front of the airway, thereby allowing the passage to remain clear (don't crush it). The restriction is then on the blood passageways and sinuses of the neck.

If a strike to TW17 or S6 seems like too much precision, then why not just seize an ear or some hair, or even "fish-hook" the cheek?

For maximum leverage sink your elbow down behind the attacker's shoulder, so that your arm acts as a bar against both shoulder and opposite side of the jaw.

The kata lets us know that the sequence can be performed with either hand equally effectively by duplicating the actions with the opposite arms.

The Gallbladder points here are the Wood points shown in the cycle diagram; should S4 be hit instead/as well then the Earth portion of the cycle comes into play. The wrist and TW points are the Fire and Metal portion of the equation.

Uchiuke = strangle + crank
Hikite = retaining hand

Sequence 6

The idea that you would block an attacker three times (marching forwards), then step back and block them again before dealing with them by kicking them in the knee is, again, laughable.

For this application to exist, the attacker must be stepping backwards. Driven back by your blocks? Simply stand still and there is no need to go forwards to the attacker, they have *left* the confrontation.

Why not perform the retaliation after just one shuto uke?

4) The fact that a technique (in this case knife-hand block) is repeated as a sequence could be taken to mean that the attack is a common one.

It could be taken to mean that receiving an attacker with your right side forwards is more effective, and that stepping in is more useful than stepping back, but stepping back can work.

More likely is that this particular defensive paradigm is usefully useable against more than one type of common method of assault.

When grabbed by the lapel, our natural instinct may be to grab the wrist of the attacker to pull it off of us. This reaction may fail us when under the effects of adrenaline. Instead of trying to use fine motor skills we may prefer to *strike* the wrist of the attacker. As Geoff Thompson writes, the affects of adrenaline will often prevent someone from using their fingers adequately, that's why the Police write statements and have those involved sign them—because if the event was recent and traumatic you are unlikely to have legible hand-writing.

So, if fine motor skills have betrayed us then no amount of wrist locking or grip removal use of pressure points will help. Adrenaline will see to it that we have reaction time but will rob us of any refinement. The movement that we are left with may appear somewhat crude, but is more useful for that.

continued

The strike should wrap around the wrist, bridging the fire and metal points on either side. Hitting down and into the wrist; the motion is also back towards ourselves— the little finger side of our hand makes contact with the delicate inside of the wrist, releasing the aggressor's intended pull without letting their hand escape. The effect of this is greatly enhanced by twisting the body. This pull may be codified to look like a "back stance".

This one action brings the attacker's neck directly forwards with their head turned to expose the delicate area on the side of the neck and the temple.

Striking this area with the forearm, approximately half-way through the *shuto* motion, we find that S9 and LI18 almost always fall beneath the ulna. As the ulna side of the arm is used for cutting rather than smashing, the twist is particularly useful.

When we analyse the "redundancy" built into the technique, we find that if you miss the wrist points you still distract the opponent; if you bring your arm up but don't strike quickly you end up catching them with your elbow; if you step forwards instead of pull you still strike vulnerable areas.

The pressure points of the wrist are engaged by our own wrist (Metal and Fire). Large Intestine adds more Metal to the equation, Stomach points are Earth-aligned.

Shutouke = neck strike
Hikite = retaining hand

Shutouke = elbow leverage
and over-balancing
Hikite = anchor point

Another look at shuto uke reveals the following:

The stepping straight punch might ordinarily fall into the realms of a karate movement, but many attackers utilise something like it. The elbow might be higher, the arc might be descending, but essentially it is the same technique. Also, look out for the one who thinks he is a boxer and throws a right cross. Should he throw his bodyweight sufficiently he will step anyway!

The end position is the same with a jab, it just starts closer. We don't want to leap miles out of the way, as if we could avoid the fight and run we would already have done so. Now what we are left with is the situation that we must control in order to survive.

When a fist jabs towards you, try to arrange your body to be *outside* the **line** of the attacker.

Throw one hand forwards to strike the gall-bladder-liver meridian crossing point. In the kata this hand is open, we suggest, to show that it only takes fingertips to "light up" the junction. A fist would be advisable. This action will distract the body's natural reactions by making the subconscious concentrate on the rib area. This naturally leaves the head and neck area more vulnerable.

Another reason for having an open hand is that the fingertips can be used effectively to dig into the CV22 point. In the situation depicted here it was not possible to engage CV22 due to the body positions of the participants.

continued

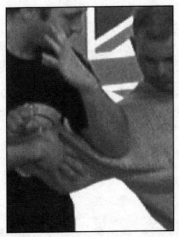

We made do with alternative positions; without thinki
about it, we just flow from one target to another c
pending on what is available. CV22 is in the sup
sternal notch, and any impact causes a "gag-reactic
that causes the attacker to falter.

The other hand parries the incoming fist *in the dire
tion it travels*, enhancing the fire meridians of t
arm. Sometimes this action is enough to make t
opponent's fist "burst" open as the energy is ov
loaded.

This jarring effect then means that the arm can
seized (preferably at H3) by the returning hand as t
deflecting hand carries over the top of the arm to stri
to the throat.

It can sometimes be necessary to change the height
the attacker by dropping the elbow down onto the t
of the arm (L5) or into the shoulder (L1), or just unb
ance them painfully by striking the elbow into H2.
any of these things are done then we often find th
the end part of the technique does not become nece
sary as the opponent has dropped before it gets the
If the opponent had not fallen we would still have t
strike to come.

No matter how tall the attacker, if they insist on punc
ing in our direction we can get our elbow over th
arm.

continu

Don't forget that the use of back-stance can be to leave a foot behind an attacker to aid their "trip".

This is all contained within the first half of the motion; what some may call the preparatory position. It does require fast work and a continuing change of hands, but the action is natural: as one hand travels forwards the other travels back; any latching is not dependent on fine motor skills but rather on the feeling of "sticking" to an opponent. This must be developed into a trained reaction.

Following on:

In all cases the front foot can be used to assist by stepping on the opponent's foot (LV2 or 3) or by tripping them as they are struck.

The "two-way action" of a high strike to the front of the body whilst the leg makes some small impact on the lower rear part of the body will again make the body's natural defences falter. Once again quadrant Theory is illustrated.

Note that the natural "cross-body motor-reaction" causes the potential continued assault to go in the opposite direction.

In a very small way, the contact with the body is following our "down the front-up the back" hypothesis.

The points which come into play are many and varied.

We have the Fire and/or Metal of the "brushing" hand, the Wood points of the GB/LV crossing; the additional Fire of the Heart and the additional Metal of the Lung; and the strike to the throat with more Metal (LI) or Earth (S).

Fire points are H2 & 3, TW11,

Metal points are Lu 1, LI18

Wood points are the Liv/GB crossing, Liv 2 & 3

Earth points are S9

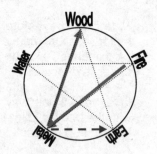

Although the kick itself has a sensible target, one does not turn to block an-other strike while our hikite elbow strikes the person we have just kicked. Note also, that the inside or outside is a *better* target on the knee than directly against the front of it.

The person we allegedly turn to block would hit us while we are kicking their accomplice.

We must ask whether the attacker would really use a stepping punch, again.

Using shuto uke to block is again better assisted by taisabaki. Note, though, that the usual application has the edge of the hand ort the wrist make contact with the edge of the opponent's wrist—this is difficult to do and only defends a small area. The whole of the forearm covers a much greater area.

5)   The kick to the knee is often used correctly in bunkai, but the *irimi* (entry technique) is often overlooked.

Once again, the only reason to use two hands upon one gabbing hand is if it will make the other weapon go away.

Our example uses a cross-body wrist grab. We do not wish to knock the hand away from us as this would bring the attacker towards us. It would also free that hand for the attacker to use again. The ridge-hand/thumb bone is used to cut through the attacker's wrist, bringing our hand past our heart.

Some people ask why anyone would want to grab your wrist. It could be that you were attempting to leave and the attacker did not wish to let you. It could be that you tried a distraction technique like flicking your hand towards their groin. It could be that you were reaching for a weapon, or even just the door handle.

In any situation, once someone has grabbed your wrist they have you right where you want them!

This is a wonderful opportunity as it is natural for the attacker to want to control you but exceptionally difficult for them to achieve this.

The sheer number of joints and their versatility means that the aggressive attacker has very little hope of preventing you from doing what you want to do.

The problem with twisting wrists (even through the smallest circle) is that the attacker is liable to let go when he feels the pain. This would leave him free to strike again. As we do not want him to have any opportunity to strike it become necessary to secure his grasp by pinning to us—we force him to hold on!

This does not have to be a tight grip, just enough pressure is necessary to keep the fingers in place on the wrist.

The pressure through the elbow makes the attacker lean away, so sending the attacker's other hand away.

Commonly, students try to use strength to overcome the attacker's grip. It is very difficult to do this way, and one should remember the easy factors which change the rules in your favour:

- Move from your hips. The whole body does the technique, not just your arms.

- Controlled pliability. Any tension will prevent the technique from working.

- No-one said you weren't allowed to move your body to the "outside" line. The attacker may have your wrist but they don't have your hara!

This does not use fine motor skills. It is more or less a slap to the grabbing hand.

continued

Double block = centre-lock

Continuing:

The small-circle and application of centre-lock may be enough to drop the opponent without the need for any further striking. Arranging the opponent into a beneficial position before the lock can be resisted; so it is codified into kata as a slow movement in order to show it needs plenty of study so that it can be done instinctively no matter the strength of the opponent.

The raised knee is often over-looked as a "preparatory movement". In fact this is used in a similar manner to the first sequence in the kata to hit the Gallbladder/Liver meridian-crossing point in the delicate rib area, enabling the kick through the knee to be that much more effective.

So far, the wrist Fire and Metal points are used, the additional Metal of Large Intestine 3 is used to keep the hand in place, and potentially we overload the Metal points by touching Large Intestine 10 & 11 or gouging Lung 5.

continued

And:

The knee is applied to Yin and Yang Wood meridians crossing point between the Gallbladder and Liver meridians. Then the edge of the foot is bought down on Kidney 10 (Water), Liver 7/8 or 9 (Wood), or Spleen 10 (Earth).

The kick will be devastating on pretty much any target. In particular, we look at the mechanical position of the "dimples" around the knee, and join them together diagonally through the knee-cap. These lines describe the direction of force for effective use against the knee.

Also of interest is the Liver meridian and its course up the inside of the leg. Liver 9 is particularly devastating and must be approached with care in practice.

Holding onto the wrist and pulling sharply doubles the power of the strike and also makes it a two-way action. Note that the pull is towards the heart.

Hizageri = rib strike
Kansetsugeri = knee strike

The last part of the sequence—a turn and face the other way making shutouke is a continuation of the movement.

Highly dangerous, this move is applied directly to the opponent's head.

The twisting motion that occurs takes the head through three different angular rotations and would probably break the neck. When one experiences the smallest jarring twist one understands that the full movement and force applied would be catastrophic for the attacker.

Most people can resist a push on their neck in one direction; the more complex the "torque" becomes the less anyone is able to resist. The technique is aided here with a change in direction for the practitioner's body.

Note that the technique is carried out working close to the practitioner's own heart. This is where we have the most physical power, the best ability to use our strength.

Instead of concentrating on the end position, we look in detail at the path that the hands have travelled through and what might be between them.

No matter which way the attacker is facing at the beginning of this movement they feel the multiple angles of the torque and risk a broken neck if they do not comply with the request to turn.

Another assistance to this technique can be placing the right foot down. This can be seen as a stamp in and down through the top of the calf muscles (Bladder 39 & 40) causing the attacker's body-weight to hang from their neck as well. Should you miss the back of the leg and place the foot down on the inside of the ankle then you should aim to scrape the Sp6 (Triple Yin Crossing).

In the kata this is written as making kokutsu-dachi (keep your weight back) while placing the foot down. Once again we see that the "stance" made in the kata is a direct application of weight and direction to application.

Shutouke = neck break

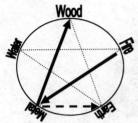

The points used include the (Yang Wood) Gallbladder cluster, Gallbladder 20; (Yang Earth) Stomach 4,5, & 6; (Yang Metal) Large Intestine 20; (Yang Fire) Triple Warmer 23; and anywhere on the Conception or Governor vessels.

Remember; just because this move occurs in a kata does not mean that it should be used. This **must not** be practised with a partner. When working on the kata it is enough to *indicate* this movement.

Remember; just because you didn't use any "power" doesn't mean that your training partner won't experience any "pain". You have no way of knowing how much your partner can take—it is better to err on the side of caution by having your partner tell you that a technique did not work than it is to find that your partner can never tell you anything ever again.

We can well imagine that any particular training partner has a pain ratio which is what percentage they can take before they become unconscious, how much they can take before something breaks, and how much they can take before they die. We have a ratio of power that varies between "no effort what so ever" and "everything we have". The trouble is that there is very little correlation between the two ratios. We have no way of knowing if our version of 5% will be our partners 75% tolerance level. As such, we would be wise to err on the side of caution in practice.

When we look at a technique like the preceding one it is easy to understand why organisations based upon sport karate do not use applications in their kata. This kind of technique is of absolutely no use in competition.

Kata techniques were not designed to be used in competition, but rather were for self defence when all other methods of placating an opponent had failed and there was no other option available.

Sequence 10

Two shuto blocks followed by breaking apart someone's grab, is again, ludicrous.

Variations usually explain that the grasping hands must be impacted upon by your rising arms *before* the opponent has actually laid them on you in order to make the technique work!

Invariably when a class practises that the grab has actually been made someone ends up knocking the opponent's grabbing hands up into their own face. Someone's strong grab will not be effectively dislodged by knocking it upwards toward your own face. Someone's weak grab can be broken by pushing them away.

It can be proved easily that pulling towards the heart is stronger than pushing away from it. A person pulling you in will always be stronger than you trying to push their arms apart. Those practising the above application are more likely to have to use physical strength than technique.

Have a partner put their arm out. Thy can bend it so they feel strong. Tell them you are going to push their hand towards their heart and they are to resist. Invariably the hand collapses towards the heart. Tell them to put their hand on their heart and you are going to pull it away from their heart and they are not to let you. You will find that you need two hands and a good bit of leverage. They are definitely stronger with their hand across their centre-line.

No muscle in the human body pushes. All muscles pull. You are more able to pull than you are to push. Pushing is pulling with the reverse muscles to the ones which pull towards the body.

The double tetsui application is not so silly, but could be better. It ignores the fact that an attacker who has grabbed you with both hands will be seeking either to head-butt or knee you, but does show a nice vulnerable effective target for your retaliation. The biggest problem with this one is that the opponent, once hit, is likely to head-butt you as he buckles forwards!

6) When hand movements are duplicated (right side and left, one after the other or simultaneously) it is often a sign that a technique can be carried out equally well with either hand to either side of the opponent.

In this case we can see that someone who has been seized by the lapels is at risk from a head-butt or knee attack.

In order to control the opponent we want them to be within our "power zone". This means that they should be close to us (preferably in front of our chest) in order for us to work on them.

A cutting motion with the ulna bone into the points LI10 & 11 will produce a violent forward jerk of the attacker's head, disorienting them enough to allow a follow up attack. The cutting motion should be towards our own heart.

When we face the potential of a head-butt, it may be to our benefit to bring that head in - but to a place of *our* choosing.

Don't allow them near your face even if you intend to head-butt them! You need to butt with the front "corner" or the side "edge" of the head. You can bring their head down into the centre of the chest to facilitate chokes, strangles, or attacks to the head; or even brought down onto the ball of the shoulder as a form of returning the shock to the attacker.

continued

As the head has been brought low and the attacker pulled in, he has been made to lose his balance: in this situation he is unable to use his knees to attack - he is more interested in being able to stand.

Some people will test this move and find themselves unable to bend their partner's arms. This will usually be because the partner has locked their arms out straight.

If the partner has done this then they are keeping you at bay - they have no wish to head-butt or knee you and so they are not "an attacker"! The attacker will have their arms bent to pull you on to their attack.

If you do need to combat a "fixed arm" just give it a small knock upwards (just above the elbow) before slipping your arms over the top and then continuing the downward movement as described above.

The supporting technique given here is a hammer -fist attack which rises into the jaw (stomach meridian) or throat (stomach/large intestine). It could just as easily be the body shift and straight punch which is illustrated next in the kata.

continued

The points of the jaw are made more vulnerable by first striking the arms as seen in the previous technique. This follows the law of reversing the Cycle of Construction by first striking metal points and following on to Earth points.

Having struck the head, a nasty wrench can be applied by seizing the opponent's ear, hair, or their head itself and pulling it down with either hand in order to make another hammer-fist attack to the jaw (assuming the wrench doesn't do the job). Remember that the more angles the neck is forced to pass through, the better, while bringing the head round and down. The opponent should be stunned by the initial strike, but the twist stops them from using any determined hitting anyway.

This blow may be brought to bear on any of the available targets including the throat, the occipital area of the skull, the ear itself, or even down and into the body.

The complex torque of the wrench is usually irresistible as it passes through many different angles. Remember, the human body can usually resist a push or pull in a single direction: as more angles are added so we find that human body (or mind) is less able to resist.

In oriental medicine we can see that we have access to fire and metal meridians, and a negative feedback into the earth meridians of the jaw, more fire with the triple warmer (surrounding the ear/back of the jaw), or wood with the gallbladder points (back of the head).

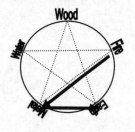

Double Tettsui = pull and strike

Sequence 10

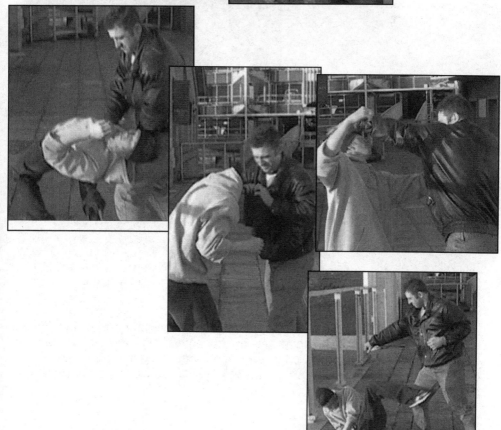

Sequence 11

The sweeping movement is often seen as preparatory and followed by a groin grab.

Males the world over have a natural innate ability (flinch reaction) to protect their genitals. Modern clothing will usually prevent the grasping of genitalia as well. The usual explanation is the product of an exaggerated ego.

Blocking a kick this way is also not advisable. Once again we have a bad resolution of the impact between *ulna* and leg (leg is invariably bigger— a well-intentioned kick will usually break the ulna).

This position ignores the defender's right hand, or, more preposterously, has the attacker punch at exactly the same time so that both of his limbs are blocked. As the attacker will usually have longer legs than arms they must either be out of range for the punch or very close for the kick. Kicks *that* close are not stopped in this way.

7) A frequent mistake when discussing bunkai is for practitioners to utilise only the end position of techniques. This occurs especially with this sequence.

The entry to the technique can be achieved from a headlong grapple/rugby tackle, or as shown here, from a jab/straight punch. Having evaded the initial attack our attention is turned to making sure the attack cannot continue.

Striking down the front of the opponent's face we can be sure of some kind of contact. We may impact the brow, the nose, the chin, or even if we miss the face and impact the body we will strike the sternum or clavicle.

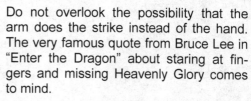

Do not overlook the possibility that the arm does the strike instead of the hand. The very famous quote from Bruce Lee in "Enter the Dragon" about staring at fingers and missing Heavenly Glory comes to mind.

The real issue with kata bunkai is the preoccupation with various body parts being assigned tasks. This is not relevant. The technique does the work, not the palm, not the fingertips, the technique. If the forearm makes contact then the forearm is the striking tool.

If the technique merely makes him head-butt your shoulder then your shoulder is the striking tool (note that the "guiding hand" should prevent your collarbone from becoming the striking tool as this would be a weakness rather than a strength.

continued

This is really a redirection of force technique: the attacker was throwing their weight and force forwards, and far from stopping it, we merely point him towards the floor (or back the way he came if you are very skilled).

The points that may be struck on the forehead, nose, chin, throat, and sternum all lie along the Governor and Conception vessels (some of the most vulnerable points on the human body). There will be a feeling of massive energy drainage, and strikes to the conception vessel should not be practised on females.

It's called the *conception* vessel for a reason!

Energetically this can be seen as a huge backwash of energy away from the head. This ki drainage leaves the head extremely vulnerable aside from the potential broken nose/jaw etc.

With a little use of spiralling hands, the strikes can be made to twist the jaw (via the stomach meridian) and also to strike down onto the top of the pectoralis (also via the stomach meridian).

The other hand is used to simultaneously strike upwards into the gallbladder Yang reservoir point GB20. This is a known knockout point. Even if the gallbladder point is missed the base of the skull (and its connection to the spine) is potentially fatal.

Sequence 11

The pulling out motion is usually explained as removing someone's gonads. This is laughable mainly due to the "flinch reaction" that all human males have, no matter what their nationality. Men move away from someone grabbing towards their groin. Modern clothing also makes it impossible to effectively grasp male genitals. Striking them is possible, but "tearing them off"? Some would like to argue that this was a technique used against samurai of old; going below the armour plates to grab the necessary area. Sorry, but even old Japanese underwear prevented any "ripping" that might have gone on there.

A worse explanation which we have seen involved a high level and low level simultaneous block against two separate opponents. Can you picture the next logical scene?

No matter how much we think that "Training, training, and more training" will enable us to handle anything there is always the issue of common sense.

No matter how fast and hard our retaliation, or how aware of our surroundings we are; neither of the attackers in this illustration have been defeated. They will land a blow; we would have to be lucky for that blow not to incapacitate us.

This technique is a follow-up to the previous technique where we have impacted down the attacker's face.

The move is a reversal of the initial impact: a neck wrench. Again it is important to see the middle position and not the end "follow through" position.

The end position is "over-kill" - an over-training of the body to enable it to perform correctly when it must function under adverse conditions (a fight).

Performed slowly in the kata, we are made aware of the seriousness of the technique, but also how much study of this technique is required.

It's worth repeating: We must note that human beings can resist a twist in one direction. The path we take here twists the neck through three different planes (two is usually enough) whilst the body is pinned in place by the attacker's own arm.

Remember, he threw the fist at you: if you choose to keep it and he can't break-fall out of the move because of his pinned arm then...

It is each individual's choice as to what constitutes a reasonable response, and what circumstances require such a response, but this explains the move from the kata in a far more useful way than making an upper and lower block at the same time.

Continued

Note once again that it is not the end position which causes the damage, but rather the *process* of getting to the (over-kill) end position.

The hand on the jaw manipulates the head via the stomach meridian (Yang Earth), the hand on the back of the head manipulates the neck via the GB20 (Yang Wood) and GV points.

The clamping of the hands towards each other, and deliberately keeping fingers away from the attacker's mouth should prevent biting, and the angle which you turn the head (jaw away from you) means that the attacker's free hand is thrown out in the opposite direction (away from the defender).

It should be noted, once again, that fine motor skills can ad to this technique, but are not necessary. If this were your forte then making contact with the forearms and performing the move would be sufficient.

Manji gamae = neck manipulation

This supplementary version of the technique uses some of the most extreme methods of unbalancing someone.

The version shown here uses the opposite legs and hands to the way they are presented in the kata.

The manipulation is carried out after having avoided a jab or straight punch, by moving in tight towards the opponent from the off-line position.

Classically demonstrating Quadrant Theory, the push works on the front and the back, nearly at either end of the spine (the longest set of joints in the body).

Pushing against the small of the back and pulling against the forehead or just under the nose (GV26) completely disturbs the equilibrium of the person attacking.

Although GV26 may be considered a small target, it is simple to locate with the web of the hand. It is also entirely natural to use the correct angle (45 degrees in and up) to activate the alarming reaction.

To make matters worse, dig the finger an thumb into opposite LI20 points (assuming you have the co-ordination/inclination).

The opponent feels their pelvis buckle out from under them, their knees projecting too far forwards to keep their balance. Worse is the fact that as this happens their head is pulled back. This isn't simply losing your balance; it's losing your balance in two directions at once. If any further twisting of the hips were added then we would see further angles attacked and further damage done.

Only the slightest touch is needed, the twist of the hips to flow *with* the attacker's initial direction of travel does most of the work.

The attacker's forward momentum aids his downfall. The defender's position is one of relative safety as to his likelihood of being struck. Note that the height of the attacker is of no consequence as their height is changed by the technique.

At the end of this situation we might choose to drop the attacker and run, we might continue to hit them or choke, or in extreme circumstances reverse the action to combine the moves shown previously for this piece of the kata.

Sequence 13

The fumikomi and gedan barai usually only fails to explain why you would want to block and move in towards an opponent.

Fumikomi here does not reach the opponent's knee at all.

Once again, the forearm ulna bone is too fragile for blocking with.

Essentially, we are observing that the usual applications only take into account a distance which is useful for *kumite*. As altercations do not generally involve kumite, but rather a vicious assault by someone with no regard for your safety or any *rules* which you may live your life by these are unsuitable if self-defence is your aim.

If this application begins inside of kumite range then the defender will get kicked.

If this application begins outside of kumite range then we see really there is no need to block the kick (even if such a thing were possible) as it is out of range. Any amount of side-stepping or shifting would be more applicable.

8) Stepping out into a "horse-riding stance" and making a "downward sweep" with the arm.

During an altercation the distance can very quickly close to grappling range. Whilst this offers a number of opportunities many of us are not comfortable with wrestling with a determined opponent.

Luckily it is natural for us, when grabbed, to bring our hands up on the outside of the opponent's arms. We do not want to be within their grasp trying to overpower them. It is better to disrupt their upper body from the outside.

This part of the kata advocates a swift knee raise, connecting with the groin or stomach. Should the attacker flinch his leg inwards we may well find ourselves striking the outside of his thigh with our knee. We don't mind—these are all valid targets, and a much better bet than trying to stop someone's kick from eight foot away.

The opponent's natural reaction will be to crease their body, so we must be especially careful of head-butts at this stage; just control how the head comes in.

Many times we see television programmes or films where a man gets kneed in the groin, usually from a rising knee. This can actually be very difficult to achieve, as most people's knees are, despite bravado, bigger than the space between a man's legs! Remember that the knee should be thrust forward as well as upward in order to properly impact. If we don't "get them" on the way up we will on the way forwards! This will correspond to the many times we are told to use our hips when kicking.

Twisting the body means that we stop trying to match strength with the opponent and plunge our foot down through their knee (LV7 & 8 or SP10). There is a saying that the body is vulnerable "anywhere the sun don't shine" and this is why we prefer the inside of the knee.

Occasionally the opponent will twist their body so much from the knee impact that their other knee becomes available as a target from the "outside". No problem, just hit here instead.

This is a prime example of looking at the situation and just "doing the kata". At this range, without looking for targets, the moves themselves are enough. The practice of the kata will find the way to appropriate targets *when distance and realistic attacks are presented*.

Fumikomi = knee strike as well as stamp.

Following on from the previous grappling application:

As they begin to fall under our body-weight applied to their knee joint, we find that our forearm is close to the attacker's head.

Striking down across the jaw-line (Stomach meridian points 4, 5, & 6) the opponent is knocked to the floor.

Throughout this tactic, the opponent is kept close to the defender. This feeling of winding around the attacker and causing the attacker to be spun around you should not be overlooked. It's that "multiple angles" thing again!

The very act of fighting back has changed the opponent's expectation. Their plan was that you would fall beneath their attack.

In this stressful situation we have responded with short techniques which penetrate through the attacker's defences and continue until we are satisfied with the outcome.

continued

Gedan barai = head manipulation

The short sequence from Bassai Dai illustrated here conforms to our wish that

- the techniques will make **contact** with the opponent part of the way through the movement,
- they occur at a **distance** which might actually happen,
- they conform to the **theories** which we judge "good bunkai" by (Quadrant, 5- Element, Yin-Yang, etc)
- and *naturally* strike **pressure points** which don't need to be hunted out - they just happen to lie beneath the techniques of the kata.

Sequence 14

The extending hand is usually seen as preparatory, ready for a mikazukigeri which alleges to remove a weapon from an attacker's hand. We have also seen this hand described as a block to an attack. If you are stood sideways on like this, at this distance, then no attack will connect enough to do any harm.

The attacker would move around and attack the unprotected groin or the open abdomen.

No reason is given here for the use of kiba dachi, nor why the outstretched hand should make this shape. No matter which side the opponent attacks with, nor which side our hand ends up on, the distance and positioning are unreasonable.

9) This very easy technique is often seen as a "preparatory hand".

Having evaded an incoming punch, we latch onto the wrist and over-balance the opponent.

The arm extends across the opponent, barring the neck and over-balancing them in the opposite direction to their initial thrust.

Also note the defender's leg position behind the opponent's leg. It is wise to have as many factors working for you as you possibly can.

The attacker's arm which is drawn across our chest is rotated so that their elbow sits into our body, not rotated down to the floor. This means that we could stop and secure them momentarily just by breathing out. The tension of their elbow against our body; the centre-point of a lever between our "retaining" hand and our "pressing" hand; can be quite a compliance tool as long as you have the "fullness of body" to achieve it.

The use of stance (dropping body-weight) is timed with the outward breath and the rotation of the wrist to bring everything together at the right time. Do not overlook the importance of the outward breath tensing the belly to make an effective arm-bar against the opponent's elbow.

continued

Of particular note is the way in which the opponent can remain upright until the final twist of the wrist is applied. This is a sure signifier of the importance of multiple angles (quadrant theory). As soon as the last angle is applied the opponent falls over!

Pulling the arm further back (as in the kata) once the opponent has fallen, applies a nice arm-bar to the opponent over our thigh. We use the stance to stabilise ourselves and apply leverage against our opponent.

The Fire and Metal points of the wrist are activated, the arm pushes across the Conception Vessel and contacts S9 (Yang Earth) across the other side of the body.

Kake shuto uke = forearm bar to the throat

The mikazukigeri used to disarm a blade wielding attacker is is not only silly but potentially dangerous at the striking foot exposes the femoral artery and nerve. A severed femoral artery will probably lead to death (remember, this is the blood passage used to by-pass the heart in operations; it has to be major).

The rights and wrongs of weapon disarms are beyond the scope of this document, but there are other moves which do the job of taking away a knife without running such a high risk.

Even if you should only use the move to strike into an attacking arm or leg we must question how sensible such a move would be. It is worth repeating the phrase: "I don't punch ankles and I don't kick heads." This is true with an upright person—our hands are closer to the top part of an opponent no matter how tall they are, our feet are always nearer to the floor (and the opponent's lower body). It is only a matter of efficiency to use the nearest weapon on the nearest target.

There will be some readers who know someone who took out three people with kicks to the head in a crowded nightclub on Saturday night. I dare say that these people actually exist but will certify that they are in the minority. It is a rare individual who can kick powerfully in a well-timed manner above the waist. Good for them! They should nurture their skill. Let's hope that they don't start teaching it as a system of self defence for everyone though, as most people will be off-balance and vulnerable with one leg waving in the air.

Many explanations of the mawashi empi make mention of the head, but fail to show how it is achieved. Others show pointless strikes to the chest.

The kata is very specific about stepping in and assuming a kiba dachi. Most applications reach for the head and pull it down. To powerfully impact on the head they may be better off stood up as tall as they can and swinging their hip fully.

There is nothing wrong with an elbow attack per se, it can be very damaging when thrown against an attacker's sternum or ribs. What is lacking from most of the applications is *irimi* or entry technique. They simply do not show how to get in and achieve these wonderful techniques.

10) The idea of moving one foot towards your hand does not mean that the action takes place at the hand.

When an opponent is placed between our hand and foot it may be our intention to make the hand and foot meet but this will not happen. There's a person in the way, after all! The final position, the hand meeting the foot, is the *intention*; it tells us where we want the power to go. Again we are reminded about the importance of "follow-through" in a technique.

From a grappling situation; we produce the space we need to do the technique by dropping our body backwards and away. Keeping a grip on the opponent will produce a leg being placed in front, even if they had started with their feet completely parallel (which no-one does!).

The hand is used to secure a grip or to strike the back of the neck while the foot is brought upwards. The foot will usually contact the opponent around the knee-cap.

When kicking through the knee we must be sure to strike at a 45 degree angle. Essentially we try to draw a path between two diagonally opposite "dimples" around the knee.

Mikazukigeri = kick through knee

If the foot strikes the shin, then this is valuable too. If it goes higher and ends up on the inside of the inner thigh then this is valuable, too. Once again we make the point that you should let the kata do its job—just do the technique, at the appropriate distance and things fall into place.

The opponent begins to over-balance as they have lost a leg to stand on, and as they fall we bring our elbow in at the new "Chudan" head-height. Our elbow strike connects with the temple, jaw, throat, or any other vulnerable area.

Remember that the strike has the other hand to provide a "base". This pulling motion means that the strength of two arms is in the strike.

An elbow to the head is a violent "demolishing" type of attack.

When we commit our weight to pad-work, for instance, we see that the elbow will often be one of our strongest weapons. The effect is multiplied by "capping" the direction and angle of the attack with our "free" hand.

This is often described as a "ricochet" as the power is injected into the target by the elbow and cannot leave through it's normal course through the head as the head has been captured. The power seems to zig-zag around inside the head!

Do not under-estimate the effects of the "swinging door" hip movement. We find that the body "slamming" in as the elbow connects is much mightier than the effect of hitting with "just" the elbow.

Mawashi empi uchi= strike to jaw

One of the things we sometimes see at seminars is the reluctance of traditional martial artists to stand naturally. They posture and "brace" so that this technique appears flawed. Several factors come into play; an attacker will not be "braced" against the technique; you will kick a real opponent as hard as you possibly can, unlike in the training hall; no-one stands with their feet exactly parallel, but if the "wrong leg" was forward a small pull will make the attacker put their other foot in front or they will fall over; we adapt as circumstance dictates.

The technique we are looking at is a momentary part of a larger scenario. In this example the attack has already begun; the distance has been closed and the grapple must be broken and the fight aborted by a simultaneous arm and foot movement. Slapping, pulling, hitting and using the feet at the same time, the defender takes immediate action to prevent any escalation of violence. All of this occurs at close range, with an attacker who is not stood still bracing uncompliantly, but in the middle of their intended assault.

The access to this technique is gained by shocking the body's defence systems by attacking low and then attacking high. The awareness of defending , or preparing to defend, the body will usually shift to the last place which was struck. This area is then braced against a subsequent attack. Other areas of the body then become more vulnerable to attack; the more distant from the original "hit site" they are the more vulnerable they are.

Points include Lung and Large Intestine for the "preparatory hand" which then shifts to Gallbladder 20 or Governor Vessel. The foot strikes up into the knee at LV7/8 (Yin Wood) or SP9 (Yin Earth). The elbow strikes into S4,5, or 6 (Yang Earth), or TW23 (Yang Fire) located by the eye/temple.

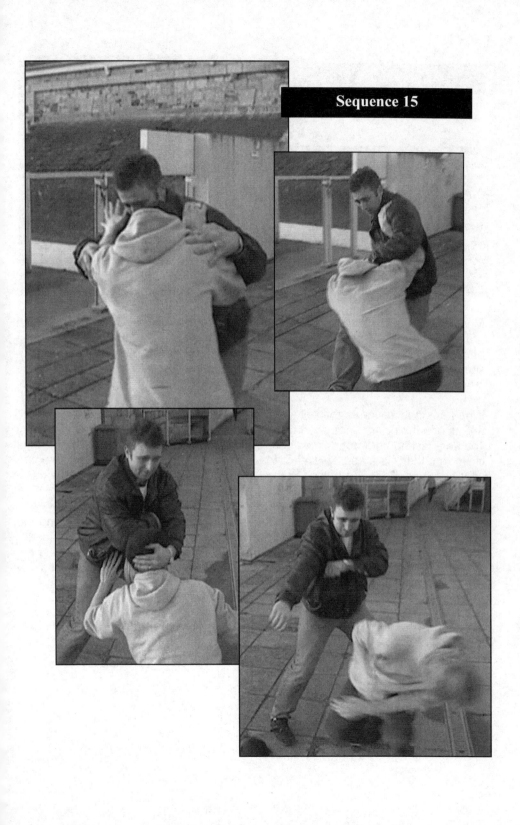

Sequence 15

Most ridiculous are the three consecutive downward forearm movements, which are mistakenly explained as blocks. Once again we see that the ulna is the area of contact. Once again we are dependent upon an attacker throwing three consecutive punches towards the same target, and once again we find that with the attacker still vertical we sit in a vulnerable position.

When this application is the only one you have then we are left once again with an opponent who has not been dispatched. The masters seem intent on letting you be attacked numerous times before they will let you strike back. Some would claim that there is a secret level of teaching which shows you "what to do next", after you have done the moves in the kata. This is not so. The kata is perfectly effective as it is, it's just the applications which are lacking.

A variant which is sometimes seen has the first fist descend as a block and the second and third as strikes to the lower body. Whilst striking is definitely better than three blocks this does not take into account the correct angle for striking the targets which present themselves when this position is adopted, nor does it show why the forearms return to this horizontal position between strikes.

11) The bunkai usually offered up for this situation relies upon an abnormal expectation of attack.

This set of arm movements constitute a nasty neck-wrench/neck-break.

This example is a response to a life-threatening assault for which you must be absolutely certain of your justification. Relating the kata to potentially lethal applications reminds us of just how nasty this art really is; and of the moral standing which must accompany those who train in it's use.

Having achieved a grasp on the head (following the previous application) we now find that either fist propelled downwards whilst maintaining a position parallel to the body with the other arm will damage the opponent.

If one twist won't do it then follow-up with another.

Note that the view shown here is a slightly "exploded" version - the distance is a little further than is necessary or likely - just to show the hand positions.

The kata informs us that our body-weight should be dropped and that we should be stable; that either blow will do but that the right hand is more frequently successful. The right-handed blow will do a better job of twisting the opponent's body away from you to prevent further grabbing or flailing strikes.

continued

Our targets are the stomach meridian along the jaw and the gallbladder reservoir on the back of the head.

It's almost as though there were a theme running through the kata, isn't it: the number of times all of the techniques can be made to land on head targets is too frequent to be coincidence.

Observe how each impact propels the opponent's weapons away in the direction of the strike. Note that the turns to the head are carried out through multiple angles simultaneously.

Even carried out at low power-levels and without keeping hold of the opponent we still manage to spin them so far that they lose track of their intention to strike us and any ability to remove themselves from the conflict.

The form concludes the set of movements by adding in a further twist which utilises a hip twist.

continued

Triple block = neck manipulation

The "cup and saucer" position informs us that following on from neck cranks with use of dropping body weight and effective targets for striking that the use of the hips may be the final straw which we need for this particular camel's back!

In class I refer to algorithms. The premise is that if formula x doesn't work then do formula y; if y doesn't work use z. This set of moves is just such algorithm of escalating complexity and barbarism.

In effect it gives us a "final factor" which may be necessary to eliminate the threat. The strong twist into what looks like a front stance adds a powerful extra power boost to what was already a nasty combination.

There is a saying: ***"Don't fight the hands, fight the intention."*** As all intention to do you harm comes from a brain it seems apt that the techniques should be able to land on heads.

Targets include TW17 (Yang Fire); Stomach 4,5,& 6 (Yang Earth); Large Intestine 20 (Yang Metal); and Gallbladder 20 (Yang Wood).

Sequence 17

Yamazuki is often seen as two punches.

Should you be able to use this your opponent would be very surprised. The question is whether you would actually do it. It isn't natural.

Presenting your face closer to the attacker as you shift within their punch/guard is also highly suspect. It brings you that much closer to their "other" fist and potential head-butts etc.

Using the arm as a warding movement whilst sliding in is not so dumb, but again we must be careful of this presentation of the ulna to deflect powerful blows.

12) Unfortunate enough to be restrained in a headlock, we must be prepared to bite and gouge our way free.

Let's face it, we shouldn't really find ourselves in this situation if our zanshin is good! Then let's also face the possibility that we wouldn't need any physical skills if our zanshin were that far evolved, and that our physical skills are only necessary because at some stage someone may get the better of our zanshin.

There are many routes out of this situation, and one must not overlook the importance of struggling to keep the opponent off-balance or biting into the delicate rib area to aid the release. Turning the head will also help to keep the airway clear.

The hand which is next to the opponent can easily reach around and find GV26 by feel alone as long as it travels over the nearest shoulder. If the opponent is big or very wide you might not get to the far side of their head.

Our other hand strikes with a hammer-fist into the bladder/dantien area (CV4). In practice this strike **must not** be performed on females in even the most gentle fashion. This area of the body is too precious to risk.

The hand under the nose must not just pull backwards, but should feed through a 45 degree angle upwards and backwards.

Notice that this application makes good use of the "pulling back" feeling following on directly from the "double punch" of the kata.

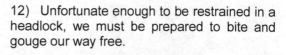

Yamazuki = high and low strike

When restrained the other way around we simply palm into the GV26 area and impact upon the small of the back/spine with the other hand.

Note how these two applications account for the "body-bent over" part of the kata. This second version also makes use of the "thrusting forward" feeling.

The legs may be added into the equation for both applications, simply raise the knee to find the "dead leg" spot (GB31) or the groin, depending on how the attacker is positioned.

Yamazuki = high and low strike

A simpler explanation is to take a "same-side" wrist grab up high.

Again, imagine that we have tried to leave a situation and the aggressor has grabbed us to pull us on to their "best shot".

The wrist of the opponent is "cut through" by our thumb bone. This releases the wrist and enables our manipulation.

As well as over-balancing our opponent this move succeeds in exposing the Gallbladder/Liver crossing and the Gallbladder/Spleen crossing and impact upwards into either of them.

Of particular note is how much more vulnerable the GB/Liv cross is when the arm is raised. Most people can take a light punch in the ribs with their arms down, but with the arm raised the whole area becomes "activated" and more easily shocked.

The reverse version of the technique is also possible: pull the wrist grab inwards and down and punch to the attacker's face. Either way you are making the shape prescribed by the kata.

Yamazuki = high and low strike

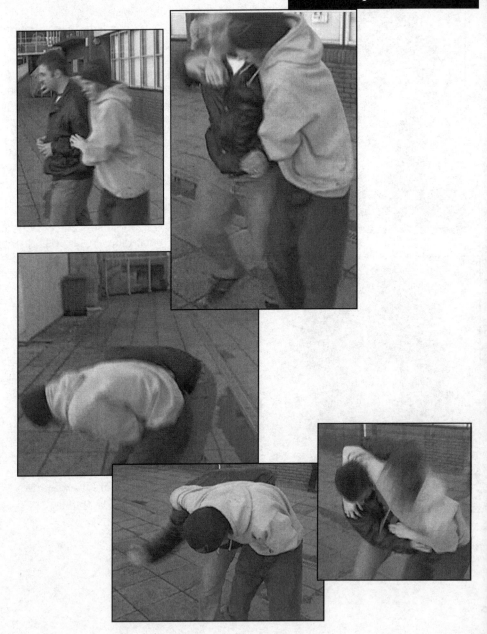

The sweeping arm is sometimes seen as connecting with a kick and then striking onto the leg.

A variation is sometimes shown as a sweep against a kick which up-ends the attacker and then the fist whips back to strike the fallen foe.

The only thing to say about this is "Try it". If it works for you against a non-karateka *really* trying to kick you then obviously this is a technique for you!

Nearing the end of this section, we find ourselves repeating our advice regarding being on-line, inappropriate limb-use for deflection, inappropriate distancing, and inappropriate expectation of attack-type.

13) During an altercation we come to realise that strength will not win through for us.

The opponent has seized us and proceeds to try to jostle us backwards towards a wall or alleyway. Their size or aggression means that any of our short strikes have fallen without effect.

Distraction striking is used to place an opponent into a position where he will not resist the technique which we intend to use.

Striking to the jaw with a "tiger claw" or a web-hand directly to the throat, we then seize and twist violently. The tiger claw would use fingers to rake at the opponent's face, a web hand is simpler, using the distance between the extended fore-finger and thumb to jamb up into the opponent's vulnerable areas.

"Going for the eyes" is actually very difficult, again because of the human flinch reaction. Sometimes you see people in films throwing two-finger strikes to the eyes, but if they miss then they'll break their fingers on your skull!

The throat seize can be a grab at the larynx if we are co-ordinated enough.

Other targets for the hand include the GV26 spot at the base of the nose; straight up to the forehead (for the evangelical "blessing") and hair grab; or directly to the ear as a

strike and grab.

The elbow may be brought directly into contact with the sternum also in this one "preparatory" movement. This elbow strike can be seen used to great effect with little movement against etha-foam pads in our seminars.

The target is CV14 or 17. These targets are dangerous and should not be struck in practice.

Having already distracted the opponent we then have the opportunity to dispose of them.

Staying in close we begin to wind the opponent around our body by shifting our hip in close and moving the feet out of the opponent's way.

The use of an opponent's balance points makes the job easy, and as soon as you include quadrant theory you have the method of moving the opponent.

We provide a hip for the opponent to fall over, and, stepping away to over-balance him, we pull the opponent down. Keep them in close. The further away they are the more reliant upon strength you have to be.

Remember to generate the twist in position from the hips, not your arms.

Note that both hands are active. A stationary hand in the kata indicates a pinning position—the opponent is already "located" at that point.

Nagashiuke = throw

If the hair is grabbed the "scoop" becomes a neck wrench. Note that this is made worse if the opponent fails to fall on to their back but instead just tumbles forward over your leg.

Throughout the movement we seek to keep our spine vertical. Should the situation not occur in the dojo then we do not wish to find ourselves rolling around on the floor where there may be broken glass or faeces, needles or any number of other hazards quite apart from any of the attacker's friends who may be stood around waiting to join in. If we go down we give them too much opportunity.

Keeping the spine vertical and the legs strong should keep us upright and aware of any potential continuation of the violence.

The follow-up "leg-scoop" is used to strike (fist to face, fist to throat, fist to sternum).

Points used include S9 (Yang Earth), the Gallbladder (Yang Wood) cluster, the Conception Vessel at the throat. Maybe GV26 and the Gallbladder cluster.

"Knee-break" = strike/neck crank

Finally there are some more shuto strikes, most with no regard for why there is a slow movement in the middle of the section during performance.

It is this lack of reasoning that destroys the image that the karate teacher knows what he is talking about. When students ask and are given answers such as "Just do it." or "When you are experienced enough you will understand."

This example is an almost mystical level of non-reasoning. It blocks a punch which is too far away to have to block; it turns to block another punch without looking first to see where the punch is; and finishes by blocking another punch from an attacker who is too far away to attack you; and all this without finishing any of them off!

This is the end of the kata. It is marked by a kiai, underlining the technique, the build up of pressure, and our warrior spirit, and yet there are people who would have you believe that there are three attackers out there that have not been dissuaded from attacking you and that the masters conclude their lesson and culminate their teachings by leaving you in this frighteningly vulnerable position.

Personally I think they deserve more credit than this.

14) We often find that human nature makes us want to fall backwards away from an attack. This is why many blocking movements are considered to be stepping backwards. This, of course, only provides the attacker with another opportunity to hit you.

We can see that moving *in* to cover an attack is preferential to moving away from it: we "close down" the opponent. Remember that the most common type of punch - the roundhouse - has a pre-scribed arc, so moving inside of the arc takes you "off-line" for the intended target area.

Moving in is also one of the hardest things to do, and only someone trained and capable under adrenalised situations should attempt it. There is no substitute for training.

The soft-block which covers the arm is thrown out into the attacking limb, often numbing the weapon instantly. Maintaining contact with the limb we pull it down and retain the elbow at our own solar plexus. This action is primarily a twist of our body and does not rely upon hand-eye co-ordination, but rather on that "sticking" feeling known as **muchimi**.

This one action exposes the opponent's throat and turns their body all in one go.

Striking Shuto to the throat, as previously shown, a potentially lethal follow-up includes moving in on the opponent.

Note that keeping the elbow down maintains a "cover" with the hand about to strike, just in case the attacker gets in another shot before you can hit him.

We redirect the opponent's momentum an use the opportunity to encircle their neck. A short sharp heft upwards here may be all that is needed to take the opponent out of action.

Despite the looping movement that the opponent goes through, we merely lead them with our hands; saving our body shifting for the final, nasty technique.

Pulling the opponent onto ourselves, stuck in a headlock, we take their head and neck through multiple angles once again. This is shown in the kata by the hands passing each other one way and then the other. It bears an uncanny resemblance to shuto uke.

The shift of the body is vital to the tearing motion which we set in progress. It shows once again that we do not rely upon the use of our arm strength, but rather on letting the technique do the work.

continued

Once again we see a quick movement followed by a slow movement followed by a quick movement to draw our attention the seriousness and severity of the technique and how difficult it is to achieve in the heat of a confrontation.

When we check the relevance of this application, and how it could possibly be related to the movement in the kata which is usually translated as "knife hand block", we first find that it leaves the defender in a very strong position, while the attacker is defeated; that the application takes place half-way through the movement as shown in the form; the application conforms to **Yin-Yang** Theory, **Quadrant** Theory, **5 Element** Theory, and the use of **pressure points**.

We can use small circles, heavy hands, we leave no gap, and we work all of the technique just in front of our heart (power-zone) whilst uniting **Mind, Breath, and Body**.

It's quite a technique.

Pressure points which may enhance our technique include blocking onto LI 10 & 11 (Yang Metal), striking S9 (Yang Earth) and LI 18; wrapping to influence S4-6 and GB20/the Gallbladder cluster (Yang Wood) and a final thrust through any neck point.

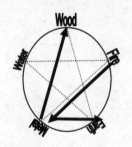

WHY?

So why do people teach applications that make no sense?

Some people (uncharitably) believe that senior Japanese Sensei held back information in an effort to trick foreigners. This is not likely. The Japanese in general do not seek to trick people. They may be private people, and they may not wish to share information with you, but if you approach a Japanese Sensei in the right way and with the right introductions then they will not seek to trick you. If they are willing to teach you their methods at all then they will teach you as much as you can handle over whatever period you can handle it for.

The most likely reason is that we have become confused as to why and how karate has been spread from the orient.

Take the time to imagine that the karate of Okinawa was taught for **self-defence** in small groups or privately. Master Itosu managed to get karate taught in schools in Okinawa at the beginning of the 1900's as a method of **fitness and attitude** programming. One of his students, Funakoshi Gichin is credited with the introduction of karate to Japan; where it was taught to large groups in the Universities.

Neither the schools nor the Universities would have had the time nor the means to teach students all of the fundamental applications relevant to their studies—but rather the emphasis was moved to creating public-spirited citizens with strong bodies and determination.

In this climate students did not have the temerity to ask what moves were "*for*". Neither were the students pre-disposed towards questioning their studies. The whole school and work culture in Japan is one of "*belonging*": you join something and you do that thing (work/play) as long as you are told to do it, and you do it because "that is what is done". There is no "*Why*?"; just "*Do*". Japanese schools spend all of their time cramming information into students heads. They memorize by rote rather than breaking information down and trying to understand and then extrapolate. Students of any subject are judged not so much on how much they know but in how much effort they apply to learning it.

After World War II the occupied Japan had to appear non-aggressive and non-nationalistic. Students of this era were taught "The Way" in order to become spiritually enlightened rather than to be able to fight for their Emperor. Many of the students themselves experimented with and promoted the sporting aspect of the art. The proficient among those children in Okinawa and the University students of Japan have grown up and spread their method of physical fitness throughout the world.

Schoolchildren were simply not taught the brutal applications which can be found in kata. How could those who were taught P.E. explain the self-defence movements to enquiring western minds when they did not know?

Another reason may be the mis-communication and mis-translation which often occurs. "Do this as if you had to stop a kick," the Japanese Sensei says. "This is for stopping a kick" is what the western student hears. The Sensei may be imparting a feeling; an attitude, rather than an application. Sometimes we just hear things incorrectly.

Recent books translate the word "uke" as "block". Earlier texts (even by Occidentals like E J Harrison) translate the term as "defence". Age uke was not seen as a Rising Block but recognised as a rising defence. Those who study the arts of Aikido and others use the term uke to mean "one who receives" implying a yield against force rather than a solid head-to-head clash.

In relatively recent times it became apparent that there were elements of the old karate which, with the passing of the last generation of old style masters, would be lost to the world forever. The last of the students who had trained in the 19th century dojo of Okinawa are passing away; and with them were passing many of the meaningful parts of our historical art.

With the War decades behind them and awareness of how openly available most information is in the current day it was time for a change. **Hohan Soken** made his *secret notes* available to **Teru Oyata** and **George Dillman**.

Researching with Dillman were **Tom Muncy**, **Rick Moneymaker**, and **Rick Clarke**. Their search for the origins and meanings of the universal martial arts inspired people like **Vince Morris**, and **Russell Stutely** here in Britain.

Russell Stutley and **Anthony Blades** have been pioneers in spreading the word about effective use of kata applications, and it is mainly from them that we have many of the keys which we use to decipher the kata code.

Another avenue of research was undertaken by **Patrick McCarthy**, searching for that "something more" which seemed to be missing from his competitive career; Kyoshi McCarthy translated **The Bubishi** (the Bible of Karate) into English. The Bubishi may be the oldest surviving text on martial strategies and how pressure points relate to the techniques of the martial arts. Kyoshi McCarthy's research also led to the resurrection of two-man "flow drills" as a means of training rather than solo re-enactions of self-defence techniques know as *kata*.

Meanwhile, a gentleman by the name of **Erle Montague** was busy shaking his head as many of these principles and ideas had long been present in the science of Dim Mak as an adjunct to Tai Chi Chuan practice. What was all the fuss about? The fact is that most of the people who knew anything of these principles weren't previously telling.

The correlation of the results from many disparate sources reveals that there are only so many ways to use the arms and legs, that some ways are sensible and others are not. What we are left with may not be Original Karate. There are no videos from the 18th and 19th Centuries. There is no way of ever knowing for sure what that original art consisted of, but modern usage should be sensible, effective, and in line with the aims that karate has always espoused. Anything less results in the loss of a lot of good people from Karate. Perhaps teaching adequate applications would not prevent the "moving on" of all of those "used to do Karate" students, but it would be one less reason for them to leave.

There is a belief in some quarters that the applications which follow are some "secret level of teaching" not to be shared with any but the most dedicated of students. This falls apart on several levels, not least of which is the loss of intelligent people disillusioned with an art which "doesn't work". It isn't the art which doesn't work, just the level of teaching.

Practitioners defending their association heads will sometimes be heard to remark that "This type of application isn't suitable until you're a Third Dan". Mentally programming a student for 10 years to make a hard block with his *Soto-uke* will stymie the student's ability to use the technique as anything other than a block. Under stressful conditions you will "***most often do what you do most often***": if you practice 3000 hard blocks over the years you will not suddenly be able to do armbars because you did it 4 times on a seminar at 3rd Dan.

Early introduction to workable applications gives the student time to mature.

Showing someone how to achieve a knock-out doesn't mean that they will immediately go out and do it! It *still* takes years of regular, focused _training_ to get the right angle, direction, and intensity for the desired result. This doesn't mean that the applications are no good as straight-forward thumping—of course they are. It just means that a technique which works on day one can be refined and made even more accurate and effective over a long period of training—making it second nature instead of something which has to be contemplated.

There will be an argument surrounding the terms Karate-do and Karate-jutsu - some will say that you only need the barbaric applications if you are practising a jutsu form. Does this mean that sword practitioners should not learn about the best decapitation technique if the are practicing *Iaido*?

Of course the spiritual/meditative practice of Karate can continue with the workable applications in place; in fact it can promote more thought and study of consequence and awareness than the sport form.

The sectarianism within the world of Martial Arts is a nonsense. We are all studying, all   learning. We are all human beings and most of us have two arms and two legs, two eyes and two ears. We must believe, then, that all methods of Martial Art work towards an efficiency with these body parts towards safety of the self and protection of the self and those important to us.

If the applications that we have de-bunked do that for you then you need to examine your thoughts more carefully. If our applications seem more correct to you then we have served a purpose, and if not then feel free to visit us or any of our seminars so that we can get the message across.

Training Methods

If you like the applications shown in this book and want to train them then there is a very real concern over safety. The things shown here hurt. They hurt when you do them lightly.

The usual warning is that one should only train under the supervision of a qualified instructor. We would welcome students to come and train with us, but recognise that not everyone can. You should train on every one of our seminars that you can possibly get to, but you also need to train between seminars.

To this end you must heed the following advice. There isn't any way around this process, there are no shortcuts.

Train with someone you can trust to treat you **seriously**. This means that they have respect for you and what you are trying to accomplish. They will not abuse time spent training with you. They will be reliable, turning up when they say they will ready to train, not party.

Train with someone you can trust to attempt to **attack** when they are supposed to, but who isn't going to "*go Kato*" on you (or you'll end up hurting them).

> Knowing that there are younger practitioners out there: Kato was the odd-job man in the Pink Panther films who used to attack Inspector Clouseau at every opportunity in order to keep him combat-ready. Invariably he got the stuffing knocked out of him. Burt Kwok at his finest!

Start your training **lightly**. It should almost be "play". When we were younger we learned mostly by play. The animal kingdom tests relationships and combat abilities by playing. What makes you think that you won't learn best that way?

When you want to; when you are confident with your technique and when you are competent with placing it where it is meant to go AND ONLY THEN; you should increase the ferocity of the attack.

Then you can increase the power that you give them back. It has to be in that order. You will be surprised how a technique that you have been doing softly and to no effect will suddenly hurt your partner because THEY have increased their power. Not you. Them attacking harder makes them get hurt more, even if you don't change anything you do.

Add in one factor at a time, aligning your feet with the direction you want your power to travel in, then checking the distance you are working at , then adding a heavy hand, then a waveform, etc

For each extra factor that you add into your training EASE UP on the power. This is vital, or someone will get hurt. As an example, we are well known for experimenting with the effects of BAR (Body Alarm Reaction). As it has been suggested that we hypnotise people into believing that it will hurt more than it really does (the power of auto-suggestion), we like to experiment with effects without telling people what will happen. We split the class into two groups. One group act as "witnesses". An attacker is kitted out with a head-guard and allowed to build up a head full of fury and steam with exercise, or sparring, etc and then told to attack/takedown a lone subject at one end of the dojo. He charges in and then there is an almighty noise, and the attacker is dazed. The witnesses count the number of seconds until the attacker would be able to resume—it normally takes between 6 and 10 seconds, during which time the attacker would be unable to stop you form doing anything (like running). When the attacker is asked what happened he swears that he was hit—he felt it. He didn't know what was going to happen but he felt the hit. The witnesses can then reveal what they saw—the defender clapping his hands *in front* of the attacker's face—not touching him!

Obviously, in the above scenario if we also played with all the retaliations you could do then someone would get hurt, so they are left for another day.

So, how do you train with these techniques with speed and power? You could do it with a partner, but you would need a new partner frequently, as no-one enjoys broken limbs and knockouts. So we are left with doing them on your own. This is called kata.

CONCLUSIONS

Well...

This brief look at the kata does not show everything there is to learn. It has presented workable applications for each movement in the kata. There are, however, at least three applications for every move, and two-dimensional pictures will never convey as much information as seeing and feeling the techniques demonstrated for real.

We have no doubt that there will be criticism of even these applications from some quarters, which is natural and *welcome* if it provides the opportunity for further research.

Note that these applications may not be the *best* application for each technique, they happen to be ones that were demonstrable and reasonably clear for the purposes of photography and with the subjects to hand.

We are often asked how we know our applications are correct. The glib answer is "Because they work". We also know that the "other" type of applications don't work, for the very reasons that we have given throughout this book. Some will ask how we know that neck-breaks and limb-dislocations can work, and then we have to take some time to explain. When we can cause pain with just a little effort, when we can do it without exertion, it doesn't take a huge leap of faith to know that a lot of effort, or the massive exertion of a full-blown self-defence situation will lead to more painful results.

Historically, we are backed up by the publication KOBO KENPO by Mabuni Kenwa (founder of Shito Ryu). Although he was writing about the Heian kata it is clear from this Karate master's writing that a step to the left does not necessarily represent a step to the left, but may be a left-sided kamae to the front or teach us how to deal with an attack by moving to the left.

Extrapolating from here we begin to experiment and check our findings against common sense and the resistance of different partners along with their logical available counters to our theories. We look at a move and ask questions. What would happen if I were grabbed? Could this move be used? What about if he's trying to choke me? Can I use a better movement if I'm pinned against a wall? Does the attack seem natural or is it a "forced combination"? All forced combinations are binned.

At the end of the technique, would I be in a better position than if I hadn't done the technique? If the opponent isn't knocked down or knocked out is he at least under my control?

The moves are tested gently first, with the level of aggression applied by the training partner incrementally increased until we discover that the moves still work but the attacker does not want to go any further. The attacker reaches their pain thresh-hold and we agree that we have a working application. The process continues with different partners of different sizes and endurance levels. Questions are raised as to the "aptness" of the move, and whether we would "really do that".

Does it make sense?

Answers which we are not happy with we put on the backburner for further investigation.

There is a valid concern that with at least 3 possible applications for every movement in the kata one's mind may not be able to process the suitable technique for the threat at hand in a timely fashion. We are asked "How can you remember al of those techniques?" To avoid the over-loading of our technique database it is a good idea to be able to use the few techniques of Bassai for as many different threats as possible. In this way we do not have to ponder which technique to use, but instead just "allow out" the technique which comes most naturally. Remember that pioneers like Motobu Choki referred to kata as styles of karate - evidence that one kata is all that is necessary. If we have only one style and only one theme or method of responding to violence then the mind should not get confused - it shouldn't really be involved. The flow of one technique to another as the situation evolves should take place sub-consciously.

So... Would you ever use any of the techniques shown here?

Some of the techniques shown within may be considered *use of lethal force - which of course is not legal.* The reason for showing these moves is not to sanction violence of this level but to educate the reader that old kata movements may possibly have contained techniques which resort to this level of threat elimination.

Just because Karate today is taught to school children does not mean that the moves were created to deal with school children's situations.

There are versions of the applications which may be less "nasty", or there may be other techniques which do the same job in a faster of more fool-proof way. That is to say, just because an application from Bassai has been shown it does not mean that it is the only way to accomplish the desired result. Any desired result may be accomplished with varying degrees of intensity. Thus; if you cannot ever envisage the situation where a use of lethal force might be justified then either practice a different application or use less force.

If our choice of technique/our favoured manner is extremely violent then we must temper our training with the philosophy that supports it so that should we ever have to use the technique it will only be in the direst of circumstances. The level of re sponse must reflect the level of threat or we become the aggressor - something which the old masters seem to agree is not desirable.

Would you want children to see these applications? That depends on the child. Probably not a good idea for a group of 50 tiny ninja, but individually, to show someone just how delicate the attacker can be, to illustrate that when someone tries to touch them inappropriately this is what they can do? Is it justified in that situation? Some say yes, some say no.

I'm afraid some decisions cannot be made for you. The fact is that children have access to television, the internet, and computer games which include the use of violence and guns and other weapons. A responsible teacher with the right attitude and the right student could positively influence the child's outlook in these matters rather than lead to their corruption. The imagery is all around us; it is up to us how we deal with it and what value we place on it.

The techniques exist. Perhaps by demonstrating the potentially damaging effects we can urge people not to use them. Perhaps we take more care in practice when we are aware of just how dangerous a technique can be. Some will say showing these techniques is irresponsible. Sharing them without a warning is irresponsible. Not sharing them when they might save an innocent life is irresponsible. That they may fall into the hands of someone irresponsible - doubtful. The study and practice required usually rules out the irresponsible.

The End

It was not our intention to produce a best techniques book, but rather to show applications to movements in Bassai Dai which work and plausibly could be the reason for encryption as kata juxtaposed with the movements that are so often seen in books which common sense dictates are not worth wasting your time on.

Within our studies we often find that there is not enough time in our regular lessons to drill a kata for performance and practice all of the applications for all of the kata at all of the different grades. This document grew out of the need to present students with a memory aid for the applications that they have studied, and reflects some of the outright indignation that some have shown when they have purchased other commercially available books on kata only to find that the bunkai shown was foolish.

Bassai represents a true system of fighting. A system of concepts and ways to subdue an opponent which are all that one needs to study to learn to fight against a serious attacker rather than a prearranged bout. If one were to only study Bassai then one could find in it everything that is needed. The movements without a partner will improve aerobic and anaerobic fitness; the moments of tension will develop and tone musculature; and when used correctly it can harmonise the body's ki flow and so promote health and vitality.

Working with a partner who pushes you to your limits but has enough control to know when enough is enough will test your character. When they are swinging a wild punch and you must decide whether you can block or duck or evade does wonders for your confidence and your reaction time. As long as you are sensible about it.

So you can get fit, lose weight, tone muscle, gain confidence, become disciplined (or train your self-discipline) - and still use correct applications.

The study of kata is an enjoyable part of martial arts study, we hope that this document helps towards each individual's study and prompts careful research and consideration for something beyond "what you have to learn to get your grade".

There is no _one_ "correct" version of Bassai making all others inferior—there are only personal interpretations. Then, none of us look and move and have exactly the same physique as our instructors, so why would our kata look exactly like theirs? Some practitioners and styles have higher stances, some have lower stances, some raise their shuto higher, some drop it lower. Any of these are correct if the guiding principles are adhered to.

There are only principles that work and those that don't.

Appendices

Bassai Sho
Point Locations
Bibliography
Glossary of Terms

...And what of Bassai Sho, the sister kata to Bassai Dai? Well, this kata is covered in another book, but the following pages show a smattering of the applications as they were filmed and some of the other pictures from the text.

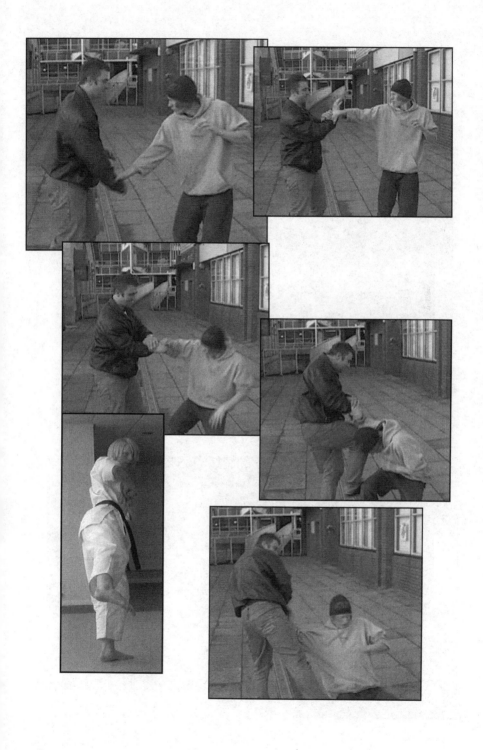

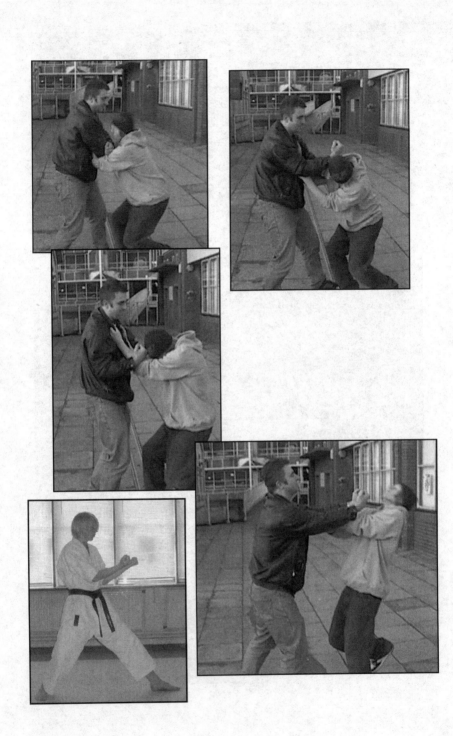

Glossary of Terms

Ageuke rising block

Bassai Dai   to storm a fortress, Major version
Budo   Way of the Warrior
Budoka practitioner of budo
Bunkai to take apart/examine/analyse

Chokuzuki   straight punch
Chudanzuki   middle level punch

Dan   degree, level
Dantien/Tanden   "Centre" of the body. In
oriental medicine just below the navel.
Dojo   training hall (lit. Place of the
Way)

Embusen   the line

Fumikomi   stamping kick

Gedan Barai   low level sweep
Gyaku- reverse/opposite

Hanmi   half-on, hips at 45 degrees
Hikite   pulling/returning hand

Irimi   entry technique

Kanku Dai   to view the sky, Major version
Karate-Do   the Way of the Empty Hand
Karate-ka   practitioner of Karate
Kata   Form, pattern
Kiai   spirit yell (lit. "everything togeth-
er")
Kibadachi   horse-riding stance
Ki   spirit
Kokutsudachi back stance

Kosadachi   cross-legged stance (woman stance)
Kumite sparring (lit. "matching hands")

Manji gamae   swastika-shaped posture
Mawashiempi uchi   roundhouse elbow strike
Mawate   turn 180 degrees
Mikazukigeri crescent kick

Nagashi   "sweeping block" (lit. "thrown")

Rei   bow/courtesy

Sensei   teacher (lit. "One who has Gone
Before")
Shodan   Level One
Shomen   square on—fully facing for-
wards
Shotokan   Hall of Shoto (Pine Waves)
Shutouke   knife hand block
Soke   Head of family/style
Sotouke   outside block
Sukuiuke   scooping block

Taisabaki   body evasion
Tate   vertical hand
Tetsui   hammer fist

Uchihachijidachi   inside of "8" stance
Uchikomi   thrust from the inside
Uchiuke   inside block
Uke   block (lt. "to receive")

Yamazuki   mountain punch
Yoi   ready

Zanshin   awareness
Zenkutsudachi front stance

BIBLIOGRAPHY

Fundamentals of Chinese Acupuncture by Ellis, Wiseman, Boss
Karate-Do Kyohan by Funakoshi Gichin
To-te Jutsu by Funakoshi Gichin
The Bible of Karate, BUBISHI by Patrick McCarthy
Torite Jutsu Reference Manual by Rick Moneymaker
Encyclopaedia of Dim Mak by Erle Montague
Unante, The Secrets of Karate by John Sells
www.24fightingchickens.com by Rob Redmond
And a special thanks to the on-line members of the KSL for the historical and translation data.

CONTACTS

www.KarateAcademy.co.uk   John Burke, Karate Academy, 8, Signal Buildings, Brunel Road, Newton Abbot, Devon, TQ12 4PB. Tel 01626 360999
My organisation, the Eikoku Karate-do Keikokai. We teach effective self-defence as found within Karate Kata. Classes are available to everyone from 4 years upwards.

www.KarateAssociation.co.uk   Anthony Blades, BAMA, 8 Signal Buildings, Brunel Road, Newton Abbot, Devon, TQ12 4PB
The association that encourages free-thinkers. There are courses throughout the year, nationally and internationally. Anthony Blades is available for seminars with traditional martial artists everywhere.

www.Russellstutley.com   Russell Stutely is Europe's leading pressure point expert. Russell makes sense of the science that is bandied about. Russell teaches effective, hard-hitting martial arts from boxers to grapplers.

www.koryu-uchinadi.com   Patrick McCarthy. Hanshi's association, the International Ryukyu Karatejutsu Research Society operate a discussion forum geared to answering historical and technical questions. The group, the KSL, were of immense help in formulating this work. Hanshi's work in historical research is without peer.

notes

About the Author

John Burke began practising Karate at the age of 11. He has dabbled with Wu Shu Kwan Kung Fu and Aikido, and enjoys finding out that all martial arts share the same techniques. In his *study* of the martial arts, John has found that there are only so many ways to use the arms and legs. He is of the opinion that style is a matter for the *individual* not lineage. In the end we must all seek to transcend style—anything less is not seeking our full potential. John was the fifth person in the UK to be graded in Torite Jutsu (Pressure Point fighting—literally translated as "twisting hand skills").

When his teacher gave up practising karate, John was forced to consider his options and, having assisted with teaching for years and having students who wished to learn, decided to teach in his instructor's place.

Teaching full-time with the Eikoku Karate-do Keikokai over four different locations has created a group of black belts who love their art and study what it has to offer. John was featured in Martial Arts Illustrated magazine in an interview; and is also the author of a technical article displaying the depth of knowledge about technique and bunkai which have led to his teaching seminars for groups from completely different styles of Martial Arts.

Seminars can be tailor-made to fit the requirements of any group. Introducing Pressure Points, Kata Bunkai, or close-in fighting and pad-work.

The name of the group "Keiko" is very special to John; it is usually translated as "practice", but also encompasses the elements of *going over the old ways*, including the all-important **waza**, **ki**, and **shin**. Together with some of the senior students and instructors John produces the Keiko Shotokan Karate syllabus on video; the Keiko Shotokan Karate Techniques, History, Philosophy, & Grading Syllabus manual; the Martial Artists' Guide to Acupressure Points; and the Bunkai video and book series.

John is currently graded in Shotokan Karate, Torite Jutsu, and Kickboxing, and is a practitioner of Iaido, and Reiki. He is the Southern Area director of the British Association *for* Martial Arts (National Governing Body) and a grading examiner for that organisation.